Designer Cards & Tags

WITH

ANNA GRIFFIN™

Designer Cards & Tags

WITH

ANNA GRIFFIN™

Fabulous Projects
Created with Style

STERLING PUBLISHING CO., INC. NEW YORK
A STERLING/CHAPELLE BOOK

If you have any questions or comments, please contact:

Chapelle, Ltd., Inc.
P.O. Box 9252, Ogden, UT 84409
(801) 621-2777 • (801) 621-2788 Fax
e-mail: chapelle@chapelleltd.com
Web site: www.chapelleltd.com

Anna Griffin, Inc.: Anna Griffin
Art Director: Holley Silirie
Project Designers: Jenna Beegle, Tracey Chabot Flammer, Debbie Schuh, Holley Silirie
Graphic Design & Production: Catherine Wingfield

Photography: Jerry Mucklow, Rocket Photography, Atlanta, Georgia
Chris Little Photography, Atlanta, Georgia

Every effort has been made to ensure that all information in this book is accurate. However, due to differing conditions, tools, and individual skills, the publisher cannot be responsible for any injuries, losses, and/or other damages which may result from the use of the information in this book.

This volume is meant to stimulate craft ideas. If readers are unfamiliar or not proficient in a skill necessary to attempt a project, we urge that they refer to an instructional book specifically addressing the required technique.

Library of Congress Cataloging-in-Publication Data available

Griffin, Anna.
  Designer cards & tags with Anna Griffin : fabulous projects created with style.
    p. cm.
  "A Sterling/Chapelle Book."
  Includes index.
  ISBN 1-4027-2004-1
1. Greeting cards. I. Title: Designer cards and tags with Anna Griffin. II. Title.

TT872.G8 2005
745.594'1--dc22
                                                                2005002183

10 9 8 7 6 5 4 3 2 1
Published by Sterling Publishing Co., Inc.
387 Park Avenue South, New York, NY 10016
©2005 by Anna Griffin
Distributed in Canada by Sterling Publishing
c/o Canadian Manda Group, 165 Dufferin Street
Toronto, Ontario, Canada M6K 3H6
Distributed in Great Britain by Chrysalis Books Group PLC,
The Chrysalis Building, Bramley Road, London W10 6SP, England
Distributed in Australia by Capricorn Link (Australia) Pty. Ltd.
P. O. Box 704, Windsor, NSW 2756, Australia
Printed and Bound in China
All Rights Reserved

Sterling ISBN 1-4027-2004-1

For information about custom editions, special sales, premium and corporate purchases, please contact Sterling Special Sales Department at 800-805-5489 or
specialsales@sterlingpub.com

Table of Contents

The Family Room in the house I just renovated.
It's good to have a room like this off my kitchen.

Introduction

You go to the mailbox every day. You sort through meaningless pieces of paper in search of something real that is hand-addressed to you. You open it with anticipation. You admire, you read, and you smile with pleasure. There are thoughts of gratitude; that is what it is like to receive a handmade card.

Finding the time to show someone that you care is something that most of us aspire to. This book offers many ideas to help you create that special sentiment. In each chapter, you will find beautiful photographs of cards and tags. At the end of each chapter, you will find simple instructions for making the projects. Patterns and templates for the projects are found in the back of the book.

It is my hope that this book provides you with ideas that inspire you to find that time, ideas that make you feel good about sharing your creativity with others, ideas that are easy to make for all occasions.

The Study is not only full of books
but full of patterns too!

Preface

One of my favorite things to do, other than making cards, is to decorate. Combining fabric prints and textures to make a beautiful room is a lot of fun for me. I have included a few pictures of my house and office on the following pages to illustrate how my love of pattern translates from my home to my work, and ultimately to my craft projects.

There's no such thing as "too many flowers." This is one of my favorite things to say when people comment on my consistent decorating element. I have flowers on chintz, flowers in needlepoint, flowers in paintings, and even on china. It's no wonder that the majority of the projects in this book are about flowers as well.

One thing that I like most about collecting antiques is that an antique instantly looks at home, as if it has been with you for years. Each piece has a story: be it a bargain, a memento from a trip, or a precious gift from my grandmother.

Combining fabric prints and textures to make a beautiful room is a lot of fun for me. There's no such thing as "too many flowers."

These passions have been the driving force behind my career. One of the first questions people always ask me is how I got started; so here goes: I grew up in my great-grandmother's house surrounded with all of my great-grandmother's antique things in a tiny town outside of Charlotte, North Carolina, called Marshville.

I always dreamed of having my own business and it is no surprise, considering that my family is full of artists and entrepreneurs. I was very fortunate to be raised in an environment where I was

encouraged and taught that anything is possible. I credit my ever-so-elegant grandmother with igniting my passion for antiques and beautiful things, which is the cornerstone of my business today.

I was very fortunate

to be raised in an

environment where

I was encouraged and

taught that anything

is possible.

With a degree in Environmental Design from North Carolina State University, my career as a graphic designer has taken me from Atlanta to New York and back. I worked as an art director in a design firm, a marketing director for a software company, and even a sales person for renowned designer Vera Wang before starting my own custom wedding

My cat, Sterling, is not too happy to have his picture taken, but I have to include him!

invitation business in 1995. The original designs and attention to detail filled a void in the wedding industry by offering a much-needed high-quality alternative to the traditional engraved invitation.

In 1996, the business expanded to include a wholesale division that offered imprintable invitations with a custom look. Brides were now able to purchase a box of invitations from a local stationery store, print them at home, and have the result be as elegant as a custom designed product. My signature vellum and ribbon, combined with the use of antique engravings, botanicals, and fabrics, were truly special and began a trend that is still popular in the industry today.

The line was an immediate success and although it has expanded to include many products, the design philosophy remains constant. I want people to look at my products and experience beauty. I want someone to receive my invitations and feel they've received a gift.

This photo shows one of my favorite collections of antique letter seals.

The product line expanded in 1998 to include elegant note cards, notepads, and greeting cards. These lovely papers quickly became a favorite with upscale gift stores, garden shops, and antique stores. In 2001, the line grew to include home office products. Beautiful file folders, mailing labels, office pads, and letterhead were designed to decorate work spaces either at home or at the office.

What inspires me in design are luxurious patterns, antique textiles and rich floral prints.

With the growing trend in the workforce to work out of one's home, I saw the need for beautiful desk accessories to enhance one's personal work space. Photo albums and guest books, address books and journals featuring hand-tied ribbons round out this delightful collection.

Also in 2001, I entered the craft industry with the Anna Griffin Decorative Papers line consisting of the beautiful papers, frames, and albums you will see used in this book. Designed exclusively for the more discerning crafter, the line fills a void in the craft industry by offering consumers beautiful, high-quality papers with a uniqueness all their own. The colorful botanical images coordinate with solids, stripes, and tone-on-tone patterns to create beautiful pages.

My designs are a

reflection of my passion

for antiques, prints,

and fine textiles.

The products also include antique die-cut frames, Victorian diecuts, journaling pages, elegant satin ribbons, and scrapbook albums. It was a natural progression for the company, as my archives of images easily lend themselves to this new category.

My designs are a reflection of my passion for antiques, prints, and fine textiles. The antique botanicals can be found on the walls of my home, while the collection of French fabrics are images taken from flea markets all over the world. What motivates me in design are luxurious patterns, antique textiles, and rich floral prints. Simple and elegant!

I have enjoyed enormous success in the last nine years. My products have been featured in many national magazines such as *Victoria*, *Martha Stewart Living* and *Better Homes and Gardens*. You can find our items in fine retail stores world-wide. Last year, we published *Designer Scrapbooks with Anna Griffin*, which was a tremendous success. Thanks to you, the demand for our products continues to grow.

The second question people always ask me is "What's Next?" The answer is always that anything is possible! I know I'll keep trying to follow my passions for collecting and decorating and making handmade crafts.

Take the time today to make a handmade card and touch those you care about the most.

As you walk through this book, and through what I call "those important moments in life," I want you to imagine the face of your mother, grandmother, sister, aunt, or friend when they open the card you have made for them. Imagine the smile, the happiness and the gratitude they'll feel. Take the time today to make a handmade card, and touch those you care about the most.

17

Happy Birthday

CARDS & TAGS

Our birthdays are feathers in the broad wing of time.

Jean Paul Richter

Remembering a friend on her birthday shows that
you care. Making a handmade card for a friend's birthday
is a whole other story! It is a gift of your time and your
creativity. Take the time to share this gift often.

Loving Birthday Wishes

Happy Birthday Granddaughter

REMEMBER When...

Make a card as a decorator would! An effortless combination of florals, stripes, and solids makes this card a year-round birthday favorite.

Coordinate your handmade card and gift tag by using the scraps left from cardmaking. A pretty tag can be used instead of a bow to adorn your gift.

FOR MY *Mother*

When a card opens and closes in the middle, it is called a gatefold. Use delightful ribbon and an ornament to keep the card closed.

HAPPY *Birthday*

Dry embossing is an easy way to create three-dimensional designs. Combine multiple border designs for an elaborate effect.

A VERY HAPPY BIRTHDAY

Sometimes tags are extravagant creations made just for trading. Make multiples of this decorative tag to trade at your next craft event.

24

Play dress-up and paper dolls all on one card!
Fancy pleats and a bow make this a perfect card
for anyone that loves to decorate.

Happy
Birthday
Granddaughter

REMEMBER
When...

Reminiscent of an award-winning ribbon, this tag
is easily made by making pleats out of paper.

Happy Birthday

CARDS & TAGS

Loving Birthday Wishes
Materials
1 Sheet of Yellow Solid (AG122)
1 Sheet of Pink Pattern (AG137)
1 Sheet of Green Stripes (AG140)
1 Sheet of Pink/Yellow Floral (AG017)
1 Floral Diecut (AG519)
Ivory Cardstock
Envelope, 4¾" x 6½"
Anna Griffin Rubber Stamp Sentiment,
    (Plaid Enterprises 2487R)
Anna Griffin Green Inkpad,
    (Plaid Enterprises 19AGR)
Decorative-edged Scissors, Scallop
Foam Adhesive

Directions
Cut ivory cardstock to 6" x 9". Score and fold in half to form a 4½" x 6" card. Cover the card with the yellow solid paper.

Cut a 5½" x 4" rectangle from the pink patterned paper, using the scallop scissors. Center and adhere to the card.

Cut a 5" x 3½" rectangle from the green striped paper. Center and adhere to pink patterned layer.

Layer the die-cut flowers for a three-dimensional effect and adhere the layers to the green striped piece.

Stamp the sentiment with green ink onto a small piece of ivory cardstock. Edge the cardstock with the green ink. You may also laser-print or handwrite your sentiment. Adhere to the floral layer as shown.

Create a coordinating envelope liner with the pink and yellow floral paper.

Cut two 4½" x ½" strips from the yellow patterned paper. Trim one edge of each with the scallop scissors and adhere along the edge of the pink striped paper, on the front and back of the tag.

Layer the die-cut flowers for a three-dimensional effect and adhere the layers to the pink patterned area of the tag.

Stamp the sentiment with black ink onto a small piece of yellow patterned paper. You may also laser-print or hand-write your sentiment. Trim edges with scallop scissors. Mat with a slightly larger piece of bright pink patterned paper. Mat this with a slightly larger piece of green patterned paper. Adhere to the tag as shown.

Finish by punching a hole at the top of the tag and threading with green ribbon.

Birthday Tag
Materials
1 Sheet of Green Pattern (AG073)
1 Sheet of Bright Pink Pattern (AG085)
1 Sheet of Yellow Pattern (AG123)
1 Sheet of Pink Stripes (AG142)
1 Sheet of Pink Pattern (AG156)
1 Floral Diecut (AG519)
Ivory Cardstock
Anna Griffin Sentiment Stamp Set
  (Plaid Enterprises 48012)
Anna Griffin Black Inkpad,
  (Plaid Enterprises 19ABK)

Decorative-edged Scissors, Scallop
Foam Adhesive
Green Satin Ribbon, ¼" wide
Hole Punch

Directions
Cut a 3" x 4" tag from ivory cardstock. Cover front and back with pink patterned paper. Cut two 3¾" x 3" pieces from the pink striped paper, with stripes going vertically. Trim the top of each at an angle and adhere to the front and back of the tag.

Fruit Basket Birthday Card
Materials

1 Sheet of Pink Pattern (AG083)
1 Sheet of Pink Pattern (AG082)
1 Fruit Basket Diecut (AG535)
Ivory Cardstock, 12" x 12"
Envelope, 5¼" x 7¼"
Anna Griffin Sentiment Stamp
  (Plaid Enterprises 48100)
Anna Griffin Gold Inkpad,
  (Plaid Enterprises 19AGL)
Decorative-edged Scissors, Large
  Scallop
Decorative-edged Scissors, Small
  Scallop
Ivory Satin-edged Ribbon
Foam Adhesive

Directions

Cut ivory cardstock to 12" x 7". Score and fold at 5" and 10" from the left side to form a 5" x 7" card. Cover the card with the pink patterned paper, leaving ¼" from the right side flap as shown. Trim this ¼" edge with the large scallop scissors.

Wrap the ivory ribbon around the card. Layer the die-cut fruit basket for a three-dimensional effect. Adhere to the right side flap of the card, on top of the ribbon.

Stamp the sentiment with gold ink onto a small piece of ivory cardstock. You may also laser-print or handwrite the sentiment. Trim the cardstock into a tag shape with the small scallop scissors. Edge with a slightly larger piece of green patterned paper. Adhere to the fruit basket as shown.

Create a coordinating envelope liner with the remaining pink patterned paper.

Trim a 4" x 5½" piece of the green patterned paper and adhere to the card.

Trim a 3¼" x 5" piece of ivory cardstock and dry-emboss the border frame from the brass stencil as shown. Adhere stenciled piece to the green patterned paper.

Cut two, ⅛" strips from the dark green patterned paper. Adhere on card front between embossed borders, mitering corners. Cut the green patterned paper to fit the center of the embossed frame. Adhere in place.

Dry-emboss the circle medallion from the bow brass stencil. Punch out the embossed circle. Mat with the dark green paper and cut out with the small scallop scissors. Adhere to the card.

Stamp the sentiment onto the ivory cardstock with black ink. Mat with the dark green patterned paper. "Hang" the sentiment from the embossed medallion with a 5" piece of ribbon. Adhere to the card. Finish with an ivory bow.

Embossed Birthday Card
Materials
1 Sheet of Dark Green Pattern (AG118)
1 Sheet of Green Pattern (AG119)
Ivory Cardstock
Envelope, 4¾" x 6½"
Anna Griffin Sentiment Stamp (Plaid Enterprises 48100)
Anna Griffin Black Inkpad (Plaid Enterprises 19ABK)
Anna Griffin Borders Brass Stencil (Plaid Enterprises 5818S)
Anna Griffin Bow Brass Stencil (Plaid Enterprises 46602)
Decorative-edged Scissors, Small Scallop
Ivory Satin-edged Ribbon, ¼" wide
Foam Adhesive
Embossing Stylus
1" Circle Punch

Directions
Cut ivory cardstock to 9" x 6¼". Score and fold in half to form a 4½" x 6¼" card. Cover the card with the dark green patterned paper.

Floral Frame Birthday Card
Materials

1 Sheet of Dark Green Pattern (AG118)
1 Sheet of Pink Pattern (AG137)
1 Sheet of Pink/Green Stripes (AG014)
1 Sheet of Floral Pattern (AG108)
1 Floral Diecut (AG521)
1 Diecut Frame (AG435)
Ivory Cardstock
Anna Griffin Sentiment Stamp Set
    (Plaid Enterprises 2483R)
Anna Griffin Black Inkpad
    (Plaid Enterprises 19ABK)
Foam Adhesive
Green Satin Ribbon, ½" wide
Hole Punch

Directions

Cut a 5" x 3½" tag from ivory cardstock. Cover front with dark green patterned paper. Cut a 3" x 4" piece of the pink patterned paper and adhere to the dark green patterned paper.

Punch out the die-cut frame and adhere the small inner frame to the pink patterned paper.

Layer the die-cut flowers for a three-dimensional effect and adhere the layers to the pink patterned area of the tag.

To make the banner, cut a 6" x 1" strip of the pink/green striped paper. Score at the following measurements: ¾", 1", 2", 4", 4¼", 5", 5¼". Fold where scored, alternating forward and backward folds.

Stamp the sentiment onto the floral paper with black ink and cut out. Mat with a slightly larger piece of the pink patterned paper. Adhere sentiment to the banner as shown. Adhere the banner to the tag.

Finish the tag by punching a hole at the top, threading the ribbon, and tying a bow.

Cut the ribbon stripes from the blue striped paper. Cut this paper ribbon in half vertically. Adhere the stripes along the inner edge of the pleats.

Cut out small roses from the floral paper. Adhere one to each pleated corner as shown.

Adhere the children's patterned paper behind the frame and trim to size. Adhere the frame to the card front. Adhere the paper doll in the center of the frame with foam adhesive.

Laser-print or handwrite sentiment onto ivory cardstock. Trim out and adhere to card front with bow. Create a coordinating envelope liner with the remaining children's patterned paper.

Paper Doll Birthday Card
Materials

1 Sheet of Blue Pattern (AG058)
1 Sheet of Blue Stripes (AG068)
1 Sheet of Floral (AG108)
1 Sheet of Children's Pattern (AG128)
1 Paper Doll Diecut (AG509)
1 Diecut 4-in-1 Frame (AG412)
Blue Bow (AGBowtie)
Ivory Cardstock
Envelope, $5\frac{1}{4}$" x $7\frac{1}{4}$"
Foam Adhesive

Directions

Cut ivory cardstock to 10" x 7". Score and fold in half to form a 5" x 7" card.

Cut a 3" x 12" strip of the blue patterned paper. Measure and score at $\frac{1}{4}$" and $\frac{1}{2}$" intervals across the strip. Cut into $\frac{1}{2}$"-wide strips. Accordion-fold the strips where scored.

Punch out the die-cut frame. Adhere the pleated blue patterned strips to the inside edges of the frame. Miter the corners.

Pleated Circle Birthday Tag
Materials
1 Sheet of Green Pattern (AG076)
1 Sheet of Floral (AG108)
1 Tag Diecut (AG533)
Green Satin Ribbon, ¼" wide
Ivory Cardstock
Foam Adhesive
Hole Punch, ⅛"

Directions
Cut ivory cardstock to a 3" circle. Punch a hole near the edge.

Cut a 1" x 12" strip of the green patterned paper. Measure and score at ¼" and ½" intervals across the strip. Accordion-fold the strip where scored.

Adhere the pleated strip around the edge of the cardstock circle, carefully turning the pleats to go around the circle.

Punch out the tag diecut. Adhere the "Remember When" circle tag to the pleated edge.

Cut out small flowers from the floral paper. Decoratively adhere them to the tag as shown.

Thread the hole with the green satin ribbon and finish with a bow.

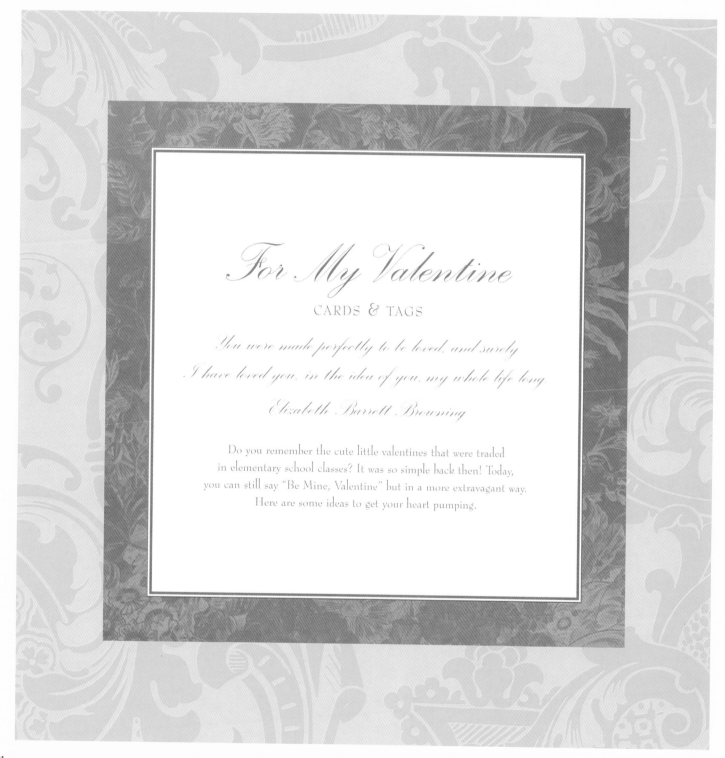

For My Valentine

CARDS & TAGS

You were made perfectly to be loved, and surely
I have loved you, in the idea of you, my whole life long.

Elizabeth Barrett Browning

Do you remember the cute little valentines that were traded
in elementary school classes? It was so simple back then! Today,
you can still say "Be Mine, Valentine" but in a more extravagant way.
Here are some ideas to get your heart pumping.

Your card can look as if you've used an antique lace doily by using a simple paper punch. Intricate edges make for a lasting impression.

Be Mine

BE MINE, VALENTINE

A

Like pieces of candy, these sweet little valentines are wrapped and ready to mail.

Here's a "fan"-tastic valentine project for all those who want to express their love in a truly unique way.

My *Heart* IS WITH YOU

Send your heartfelt wishes inside this handwoven heart. Pretty enough to be a box of candy, this card is almost as special as your loved ones.

Trim a heart shape out of the red patterned paper. Repeat the paper punch across two 1" x 12" strips of the ivory paper. Pleat the punched paper along the edge of the heart, adhering it to the back of the heart as you go.

Handwrite or laser-print your sentiment onto ivory cardstock and trim out in a heart shape. Mat this heart with the bright pink paper and trim the edge with the pinking scissors. Adhere to the larger red heart.

Adhere the finished heart to the card front. Create a coordinating envelope liner with the remaining red patterned paper.

For My Valentine

CARDS & TAGS

Be Mine, Valentine
Materials
1 Sheet of Bright Pink Pattern (AG085)
1 Sheet of Red Pattern (AG157)

Ivory Paper
Ivory Cardstock
Anna Griffin Border Paper Punch
   (Plaid Enterprises 60FLB)
Decorative-edged Scissors, Pinking
Foam Adhesive

Directions
Cut ivory cardstock to 9" x 6". Score and fold in half to form a 4½" x 6" card. Cut the bright pink paper to 4½" x 6" and trim slightly smaller with the pinking scissors. Adhere to the card front.

My Secret Valentines
Materials
1 Sheet of Floral (AG108)
1 Sheet of Pink Pattern (AG137)
1 Sheet of Pink Floral (AG012)
1 Sheet of Pink Stripes (AG142)
1 Sheet Bright Pink Pattern (AG085)
Green Alphabet Stickers (AG633)
Anna Griffin Heart Paper Punch
   (Plaid Enterprises 45HFL)
Ivory Cardstock
Ivory Satin Ribbon
35mm Slide Case
Foam Adhesive

Directions
For the valentine card, trim ivory cardstock to 6" x 3". Score and fold in half to form a 3"-square card. Cover the card with the floral paper. Cover the slide case with the pink patterned paper. Laser-print sentiment on ivory cardstock. Trim to fit in the slide case.

Wrap the ivory ribbon around one side of the slide case and adhere the case to the card. Write your secret message inside the card and wrap the ribbon around the card, securing behind the slide case on the other side. Finish with a cut-out flower from the floral paper.

For the card with a heart, trim ivory cardstock to 2½" x 4½". Trim the pink floral to 2" x 4½" and adhere to the center of the cardstock. Trim a ¾" x 4½" strip of the pink striped paper. Adhere to the center of the pink floral paper. Score and fold the layered cardstock at 1½" and 3¾" from the top of the strip.

Punch a heart design from the pink patterned paper and trim out in a heart shape as shown. Mat with ivory and bright pink paper and trim with the pink-

ing scissors. Adhere heart to the card flaps to close.

To create the monogram, trim a 5" square from the ivory cardstock and one from the pink patterned paper. Punch a heart design from each side of the pink patterned paper and adhere the paper to the cardstock square. Cut a 1" square away from each corner; score and fold the flaps that remain. Close the card like a boxtop. Adhere the flaps in place with a monogrammed circle tag as shown.

Stack the panels together and mark the placement for the bottom hole. Punch each panel with the larger hole punch in the same place. Thread the 1"-wide ivory ribbon through all of the panels and tie in a bow.

On each panel, mark a spot about 2" up from the bottom hole with a pencil and punch a ⅛" hole in the center of the panel. Stack the panels together and thread ¼"-wide ribbon through them.

Anchor one end of the ribbon to the top blade, then spread the fan open. Anchor the other end of the ribbon to the back of the fan. Adhere the remaining bright pink squares to the first and last panels of the fan to cover the exposed ribbon ends.

Print your sentiments or lettering onto ivory cardstock and cut into small squares. Add these to the fan on top of the pink squares.

Valentine Fan
Materials
2 sheets of Pink Pattern (AG082)
2 sheets of Bright Pink Pattern (AG085)
Ivory Cardstock
Decorative Square Paper Punch
Small Hole Punch, ⅛"
Small Hole Punch, ¼"
Ivory Satin Ribbon, ¼" wide
Ivory Satin Ribbon, 1" wide

Directions
On ivory cardstock, draw seven fan panels and cut them out.

Cover each of these pieces with the two pink patterned papers, one on each side.

Punch 21 bright pink patterned paper squares. Add three of them to each panel of the fan, allowing the top squares to bleed off the top of the panels as shown. Do not adhere the squares to the first or last fan panel.

Woven Heart Valentine
Materials

1 Sheet of Pink Pattern (AG013)
1 Sheet of Red Pattern (AG162)
Ivory Cardstock
Anna Griffin Sentiment Stamp Set
   (Plaid Enterprises 2488R)
Anna Griffin Crimson Inkpad,
   (Plaid Enterprises 19ABG)
Ivory Satin Ribbon, ¼" wide
Decorative-edged Scissors, Large Scallop

Directions

Cut eleven ½" x 10" strips from pink and red patterned papers. Weave these strips together tightly, with the pink strips going horizontally and the red strips going vertically. Start with a right angle, overlapping a pink strip over a red strip to begin the weaving.

Add a red strip vertically, anchoring it under the pink strip. Add a second pink piece horizontally, anchoring the end under the first red strip, but overlapping the second red piece. The weaving continues in this manner for the remaining strips, alternating red and pink strips. Anchor the ends of all the papers securely.

Cut a piece of ivory cardstock into a heart shape about 4½" tall. Adhere the ivory cardstock onto the back of the woven piece on a diagonal. Trim the weaving around the heart shape.

Cut a 5" x 10" piece from ivory cardstock. Score and fold in half to form a 5"-square card. Adhere the woven heart onto this, centering it carefully. Cut this card into a heart shape, using scallop scissors and making sure to keep the folded edge connected.

Cut a smaller heart shape from the pink patterned paper. Stamp sentiment in crimson ink onto the smaller heart. Mat this heart with ivory cardstock and trim the cardstock with the same decorative scissors. Adhere this heart to the center of the woven heart.

Add a small bow of ivory ribbon to the top of the smaller heart.

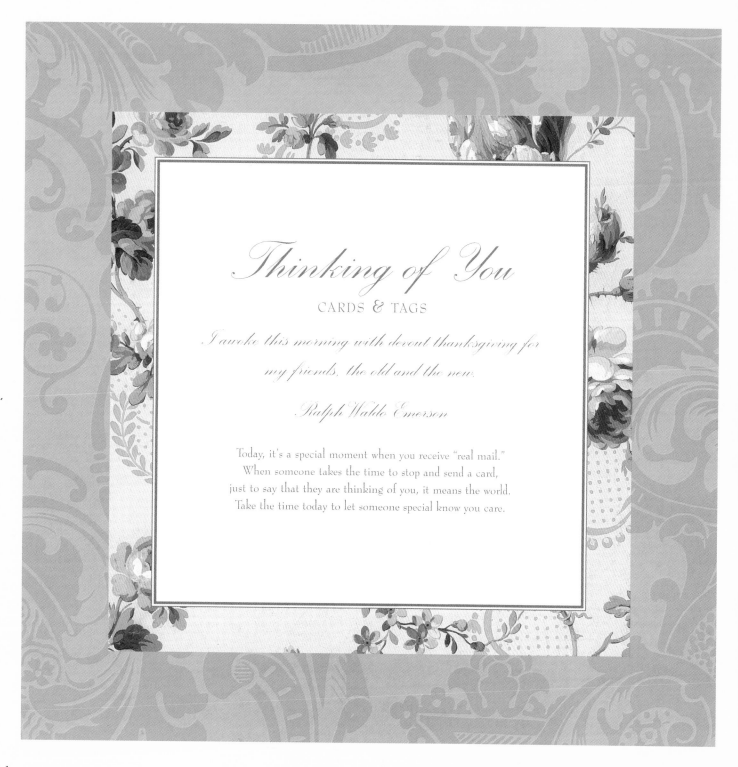

Thinking of You

CARDS & TAGS

I awoke this morning with devout thanksgiving for my friends, the old and the new.

Ralph Waldo Emerson

Today, it's a special moment when you receive "real mail."
When someone takes the time to stop and send a card,
just to say that they are thinking of you, it means the world.
Take the time today to let someone special know you care.

Tie this tag to something really special to serve as a reminder that you are not alone. Tags can be used as bookmarks, package decorations, and even as cards.

Thinking of You

*You are always
in my thoughts*

A French memo-board-inspired card is easy to make with
a few strips of paper. Your greeting and embellishment
tuck inside the strips as a finishing touch.

This tag says it all in a sincere and elegant way. Slip it into a suitcase for that special touch that shows just how much you care.

I
Miss
You

Scraps of paper can be pieced together as a background for a card. Cut four the same size for a tailored look, or use different sized scraps to create a collage.

Thinking of You

49

A tag and a card combined make this project a work of art. An embossed tag slides easily out of the vellum sleeve to deliver your message.

MY THOUGHTS
ARE WITH YOU
Always

Handwrite or laser-print your sentiment onto ivory cardstock and trim out. Mat this piece with a slightly larger piece of pink patterned paper. Adhere to the tag, on top of the roses.

Punch a hole at the top of the tag and knot the green silk ribbon to finish.

Thinking of You

CARDS & TAGS

Floral Tag
Materials
1 Sheet of Floral Pattern (AG108)
1 Sheet of Pink Pattern (AG137)

Ivory Cardstock
Green Satin Ribbon
Foam Adhesive
Hole Punch

Directions
Create 2½" x 6" tag shape from the ivory cardstock. Mat this tag with a slightly larger piece of the floral paper.

Trim out approximately twelve rose clusters from the remaining floral paper. Adhere rose clusters around the tag.

Lightly mark the center of the card at the top and bottom, and at the left and right. Connect these marks with the pencil, forming a diamond shape on top of the X. Adhere the green stripes to all the pencil lines. Trim away any overhanging edges.

Layer the die-cut flowers for a three-dimensional effect and adhere to the card.

Handwrite or laser-print your sentiment onto ivory cardstock and trim out. Mat with a slightly larger piece of floral paper and trim with the scallop scissors. Adhere to the flowers.

Create a coordinating envelope liner with the floral paper.

Memo Board Card
Materials
1 Sheet of Green Stripes (AG004)
1 Sheet of Floral Pattern (AG108)
1 Sheet of Green Pattern (AG118)
1 Sheet of Dark Green Pattern (AG138)
1 Floral Diecut (AG521)
Ivory Cardstock
Envelope, 7¼" x 5¼"
Decorative-edged Scissors, Mini Scallop
Foam Adhesive

Directions
Cut ivory cardstock to 10" x 7". Score and fold in half to form a 5" x 7" card. Cover the card with the green patterned paper, leaving a small edge of ivory cardstock exposed.

Cut out six strips from the green striped paper. With a pencil and ruler, draw two lines from corner to corner on the face of the card. This will make an X in the center of the card.

Flowers & Bows Tag
Materials
1 Sheet of Blue Floral (AG065)
1 Sheet of Green/Blue Stripes (AG066)
1 Sheet of Green/Blue Pattern (AG067)
Ivory Cardstock
Gold Cord
Hole Punch
Foam Adhesive

Directions
Create a 2½" x 6" tag shape with the ivory cardstock. Cover with a piece of the green and blue patterned paper.

Trim out four strips from the blue and green striped paper. Adhere the strips around the tag as shown, mitering the corners.

Handwrite or laser-print your sentiment onto the ivory cardstock and trim into a small tag shape.

Cut out the bow and flowers from the blue floral paper. Adhere, along with the sentiment, to the tag.

Punch a hole at the top of the tag. Create a loop with the gold cord and thread through the hole to finish.

Layer the die-cut hydrangea for a three-dimensional effect and adhere to the card.

Handwrite or laser-print your sentiment onto ivory cardstock. Trim out with scallop scissors and adhere to the hydrangea. Finish with a small bow of green satin ribbon.

Create a coordinating envelope liner with the green patterned paper.

Hydrangea Card
Materials
1 Sheet of Green Solid (AG016)
1 Sheet of Blue Pattern (AG058)
1 Sheet of Green Pattern (AG076)
1 Hydrangea Diecut (AG520)
Ivory Cardstock
Envelope, 6½" x 4¾"
Decorative-edged Scissors, Mini Scallop
Green Satin Ribbon, ¼" wide

Directions
Cut ivory cardstock to 9" x 6". Score and fold in half to form a 4½" x 6" card. Cover with green solid paper.

Trim a 5½" x 4" piece of the blue patterned paper. Adhere to the center of the card. Trim out two 2¾" x 2" pieces of the green patterned paper. Adhere to the blue patterned paper in opposite corners as shown.

Vellum Sleeve Card
Materials

1 Sheet of Green Pattern (AG038)
1 Sheet of Green Vellum (AG240)
1 Blue Rose Diecut (AG536)
Ivory Cardstock
Envelope, 6½" x 4¾"
Anna Griffin Oval Frame Brass Stencil
    (Plaid Enterprises 46680)
Anna Griffin Sentiment Stamp
    (Plaid Enterprises 2488R)
Anna Griffin Black Inkpad,
    (Plaid Enterprises 19ABK)
Embossing Stylus
Hole Punch
Green Satin Ribbon, ½" wide
Foam Adhesive
Vellum Adhesive

Directions

Cut ivory cardstock to 9" x 6¼". Score and fold in half to make a 4½" x 6¼" card. Cover the card with the green patterned paper.

To make the vellum sleeve, cut vellum to 8½" x 6¼". Score ½" up from the bottom and ½" from the left side to make flaps. Score again 4½" from the left side. Fold into sleeve, trimming excess flaps as necessary. Adhere along flaps. Cut a small half-circle at the top as shown. Adhere sleeve to the card front.

Layer the die-cut roses for a three-dimensional effect and adhere the layers to the vellum sleeve.

Trim ivory cardstock to 3¾" x 5½" and dry-emboss cardstock, using the oval frame brass stencil. Stamp sentiment in the center with the black ink. Add remaining rose diecut. Punch hole at top and add a knot of green satin ribbon. Insert into sleeve.

Create a coordinating envelope liner with the green patterned paper.

Thank You

CARDS & TAGS

Gratitude bestows reverence,
allowing us to encounter everyday epiphanies,
those transcendent moments of awe that
change forever how we experience life and the world.

John Milton

A handmade card or tag marks a special occasion or gift
with the utmost style. Express your feelings of gratitude in
a warm and gracious way with the following projects.

A twist on a traditional gatefold card, these points are reminiscent of an envelope. Wrap your expression in beautiful decorative papers.

You Are So Thoughtful

String together multiple tags with ribbon.
You can say "thank you" in many different ways.

A pretty pocket holds a photo: the perfect way to say "thank you for being in my wedding" or for whatever you are grateful.

Thank You

Woven strips of paper create a mosaic-inspired background for a card. A tag applied to the front is a pretty way to say "thanks."

Fragments and pieces of patterned paper combine easily to make a backdrop for this bright and happy thank-you note.

Thank You

On the left and right flaps, measure and mark 1" out from the fold. With a pencil, draw a light vertical line. On each flap, measure and mark 2¾" down from the top. Cut from the 1" mark to the 2¾" mark to form a pointed flap on each side of the card.

Trace the open card shape onto the blue patterned paper. Mark ⅛" slightly smaller than the card shape and cut out. Adhere the blue patterned paper to the card. Refold where scored.

Cut a 1¼"-square window out of the front flap of the card as shown. Trim out a flower from the floral paper and adhere inside the window.

Handwrite or laser-print your sentiment onto ivory cardstock and trim out. Adhere sentiment and a small bow as shown.

Create a coordinating envelope liner with the floral paper.

Thank You

CARDS & TAGS

Floral Window Card
Materials
1 Sheet of Blue Pattern (AG055)
1 Sheet of Floral Pattern (AG104)
1 Sheet of Green Pattern (AG151)
Ivory Cardstock, 12" x 12"

Envelope, 5¾" x 4¼"
Green Gingham Ribbon
Foam Adhesive

Directions
Cut ivory cardstock to 11½" x 5½". Score and fold 3¾" in from each side to form a 4" x 5½" card. Cover the card with the green patterned paper. Cover the inside of the card with the floral paper.

Cut out four 4¼" x 1¾" pieces of ivory cardstock. On one, spell out the words "For You," using alphabet stickers. Mat this onto a 4½" x 2" piece of pink patterned paper and attach to the front of the outer tag.

Handwrite or laser-print your sentiments onto the other three pieces. Mat with floral paper and adhere to the inner tags.

Insert the inner tags into the outer tags, with the top edges of all the tags meeting and with all the tags centered.

Place a hole in the top of all the tags, so that the holes line up. Set an eyelet through all the tags, but set it loosely so that the inner tags can pivot out.

Thread the pink ribbon through the eyelet in the tags and finish with a knot.

Thank You Tag Fan
Materials
1 Sheet Floral Paper (AG104)
1 Sheet Pink Pattern Paper (AG137)
Green Alphabet Stickers (AG633)
Ivory Cardstock
³⁄₁₆" Eyelet
Eyelet Setter
Pink Wire-edged Ribbon, 12"
Embossing Stylus

Directions
For the inner tags, cut four 2⅜" x 5¼" tag shapes from ivory cardstock.

The outer tag wraps around three inner tags. To make the outer tag, cut one long strip 2½" x 11¼" from the floral paper. Score the paper 5½" in from each of the short sides. Fold the paper along these lines. These are the folds where the outer tag will wrap around the inner tags.

Pocket Card
Materials
1 Sheet of Floral Pattern (AG012)
1 Sheet of Pink Solid (AG015)
1 Sheet of Pink Pattern (AG054)
1 Sheet of Pink Stripes (AG086)
1 Floral Diecut (AG525)
Ivory Cardstock
Envelope, 5¾" x 4¼"
Foam Adhesive
Photos and/or Memorabilia
Decorative-edged Scissors, Scallop

Directions
Cut the pink striped paper to 8½" x 11". Fold in half to 8½" x 5½". Fold in half again to 4¼" x 5½". Unfold and lay flat with the pattern facing up. Fold the upper-right corner behind itself to meet the center fold. This will form the pocket on the front of the card.

Refold the pink striped paper in half to 8½" x 5½". Cut out a 4¼" x 5½" piece of pink patterned paper. Adhere inside the "pocket" and adhere the folded card in place. Refold in half again to 4¼" x 5½".

Layer the die-cut flowers for a three-dimensional effect and adhere to the card.

Handwrite or laser-print your sentiment onto the ivory cardstock and trim into a small tag shape. Edge with the scallop scissors and adhere to the card.

Insert photos and memorabilia into the card's pocket. Create a coordinating envelope liner with the floral paper.

the ends of one strip of each pattern at the top-left corner of the paper, forming a right angle. Lay all of the vertical pieces across the paper.

Add all of the horizontal pieces, alternating patterns by weaving each strip through the vertical pieces. Weave as tightly as possible so that the finished weaving will be square. Adhere all ends and trim to 5" x 7." Adhere to the card.

Cut out a 2½" x 5¼" tag shape from the green patterned paper. Mat with a slightly larger piece of dark pink patterned paper.

Layer the die-cut camellia for a three-dimensional effect and adhere the layers to the tag. Adhere the tag to the card.

Handwrite or laser-print your sentiment onto ivory cardstock. Trim out with the scallop scissors and adhere to the camellia. Finish with a small pink bow.

Create a coordinating envelope liner with the dark pink patterned paper.

Camellia Card
Materials
1 Sheet of Green Pattern (AG003)
1 Sheet of Dark Pink Pattern (AG085)
1 Sheet of Pink Pattern (AG125)
1 Sheet of Pink Stripes (AG142)
1 Camellia Diecut (AG513)
Ivory Cardstock
Ivory Paper
Envelope, 7¼" x 5¼"
Decorative-edged Scissors, Mini Scallop
Pink Ribbon, ¼" wide
Foam Adhesive

Directions
Cut ivory cardstock to 10" x 7". Score and fold in half to form a 5" x 7" card.

For the woven mat, cut out eight 1" x 5" pieces of the pink striped paper. Cut out five 1" x 7" pieces of the pink patterned paper.

Stack the pink patterned pieces vertically to the left of a piece of ivory paper, and stack the pink striped pieces horizontally at the top of the paper. Adhere

Pink Thank You Note
Materials
1 Sheet of Pink Floral (AG144)
1 Sheet of Pink Stripes (AG149)
1 Sheet of Dark Pink Pattern (AG150)
Ivory Cardstock
Envelope, 6½" x 4¾"
Foam Adhesive

Directions
Cut ivory cardstock to 9" x 6¼". Score and fold in half to create a 4½" x 6¼" card. Cover card with the pink striped paper.

Cut a 9" x 2" piece of the pink floral paper and adhere to the bottom of the card. Cut two 9" x ¼" strips of dark pink patterned paper and adhere to the floral piece.

Cut out several paisley flowers, then decoratively layer and adhere them onto the card as shown.

Handwrite or laser-print your sentiment onto ivory cardstock. Trim out into a 1½" square. Mat with a slightly larger

piece of dark pink patterned paper. Adhere to the card. Allow one diecut flower to overlap the sentiment.

Create a coordinating envelope liner with the dark pink patterned paper.

Best Wishes & Congratulations

CARDS & TAGS

We are the music makers
and we are the dreamers of dreams.
Arthur O'Shaughnessy

Whether celebrating a wedding, a new baby, or even a promotion, sending
your best wishes is a lovely way to commemorate a special occasion.

ITS A *Girl!*

Congratulations
on your wedding day.

Congratulations

Just like at the altar, the bride and groom are side by side on this handmade card of congratulations.

Reminiscent of the wedding invitation itself, this handmade card wishes the happy couple congratulations in style.

A lovely way to commemorate a wedding
is to monogram a scrapbook page with
tags made for the bride and groom.

Perfect for an annnouncement of any kind, initials and monograms are a way to personalize your creations with ease.

ITS A *Girl!*

There's nothing like the birth of a baby to bring out the crafter in everyone. Create birth announcements for a friend in this simple elegant way.

Handmade cards aren't just for girls:
baby boys deserve them, too.

This cute tag is great to make for a
shower gift, or attach it to a birthday
gift for a little one.

Best Wishes & Congratulations

CARDS & TAGS

Bride & Groom Card
Materials

1 Sheet of Green Pattern (AG003)
1 Sheet of Platinum Pattern (AG006)
1 Sheet of Green Pattern (AG076)
1 Sheet of Blue Pattern (AG178)
1 Sheet of Pink/Yellow Floral (AG017)
1 Paper Doll Bride Diecut (AG503)
1 Paper Doll Groom Diecut (AG501)
Ivory Cardstock, 12" x 12"
Envelope, 7¼" x 5¼"
Anna Griffin Blue Silk Ribbon, 4mm
  (Plaid Enterprises)
Anna Griffin Green Silk Ribbon, 4mm
  (Plaid Enterprises)
Embroidery Needle
Foam Adhesive

Directions

Cut ivory cardstock to 11½" x 7". Cover one side of the card with the platinum paper and the other side with the green patterned paper. With the green side facing up, score at ¾", 3¼", 8", and 10¼". Fold where scored to form a 5" x 7" gatefold card with flaps as shown.

Unfold card. Cut an 11½" x 5¾" piece of the blue patterned paper and adhere to the platinum paper. Cut an 11½" x 3" piece of green patterned paper. Mat with a slightly larger piece of the remaining platinum paper and adhere to the blue patterned paper. Fold card.

Punch out the die-cut paper dolls. With the embroidery needle, pierce the clothing where the ribbon flowers will go.

Feed the ribbon through the cardstock layers with the needle. Create the ribbon flowers by making small knots with the ribbon. Secure the ribbon ends in the back. Layer and adhere the paper dolls to the card front.

Create a coordinating envelope liner with the green patterned paper.

Cut a ¾" x 12" stripe from the cream striped paper. Adhere the stripe along the edges of the sleeve as shown.

Layer the die-cut flowers for a three-dimensional effect and adhere flowers on the front of the sleeve.

Handwrite or laser-print your sentiment on ivory cardstock. Cut out and adhere to the front of the sleeve with a small gold bow.

Cut a 4½" x 6¼" piece of ivory cardstock. Handwrite or laser-print your sentiment on this piece. Punch a hole at the top and thread with the gold ribbon. Tie the ribbon in a loose knot to finish inner card.

Congratulations Sleeve
Materials
1 Sheet of Platinum Pattern (AG073)
2 Sheets of Cream Stripes (AG008)
1 Floral Diecut (AG538)
Ivory Cardstock
Envelope, 7¼" x 5¼"
Foam Adhesive
Gold Satin Ribbon, 1" wide
Gold Bow (RC212)
Hole Punch

Directions
Cut an 11" x 7" piece from the platinum patterned paper. Cover the back with the cream striped paper.

With the striped side facing up, score and fold the paper 3" from the left side, and 3" from the right side. Fold back the top-right corner of the left flap and the top-left corner of the right flap to form the V-shaped opening. Adhere the flaps in place, then adhere the sleeve closed at the bottom.

Monogrammed Wedding Page
Materials
2 Sheets of Platinum Pattern (AG803)
2 Sheets of Platinum Floral (AG089)
2 Sheets of Gold Pattern (AG027)
1 Sheet Cream Pattern (AG155)
1 Sheet Platinum Stripes (AG008)
1 Grey Journaling Page (AG243)
1 Platinum Frame (AG414)
2 Platinum Bows (RC210)
Ivory Cardstock
Anna Griffin Alphabet Stamp Set
    (Plaid Enterprises 48074)
Anna Griffin Platinum Inkpad
    (Plaid Enterprises 19ASL)
Foam Adhesive

Directions
For the scrapbook page, cut cream patterned paper to a 10½" square. Mat with a slightly larger piece of gold patterned paper and adhere this to a full sheet of platinum patterned paper.

Cut four 9½" x 1" strips from the platinum patterned paper. Adhere to form a frame on top of the cream patterned paper. Miter the corners.

Cut four ⅞" stripes from the platinum striped paper. Attach these to the inside edge of the platinum frame. Miter the corners where they overlap.

Add photo to the die-cut frame. Mat with a slightly larger piece of gold patterned paper. Attach framed photo to the page.

Handwrite or laser-print journal caption onto the journaling block. Cut out and adhere to the page.

For the tags, stamp initials onto 1" squares of ivory cardstock, using platinum ink. Set aside. Cut out two tags and several flowers from the platinum patterned paper.

Layer the stamped letters and the extra flowers onto the tag shapes. Use different heights of foam adhesive for a more dramatic effect. Add platinum bows to the top of the tags. Mat tags with gold patterned paper and adhere to the page.

Cut a slightly larger oval of the platinum patterned paper with zigzag scissors. Adhere the stamped oval to the decorative-edged oval.

Cut platinum patterned paper into five 1" x 12" strips. Apply adhesive to the back edges of the oval frame. Apply the strips of paper to the back of the frame, pleating the paper every ½" and turning it as you move around the oval frame.

Wrap a strip of ribbon across the rectangular frame, securing the ends on the back of the card.

Adhere the pleated oval frame to the top of the ribbon. Adhere the monogrammed piece to the top of the oval frame.

Create a coordinating envelope liner with the remaining platinum patterned paper.

Monogrammed Card
Materials
1 Sheet Platinum Pattern (AG089)
1 Platinum Diecut Frame (AG414)
1 Oval Frame (AG434)
Anna Griffin Alphabet Stamp Set
   (Plaid Enterprises 48075)
Anna Griffin Platinum Inkpad
   (Plaid Enterprises 19ASL)
Platinum Satin Ribbon, 1" wide
Ivory Cardstock
Envelope, 7¼" x 5¼"

Decorative-edge Scissors, Zigzag
Foam Adhesive

Directions
Cut ivory cardstock to 10" x 7". Score and fold in half to form a 5" x 7" card. Cover the front of the card with the platinum frame.

Remove the center from the oval frame. Use platinum ink to stamp monogram onto the reverse side of the center oval.

It's A Girl! Card
Materials
1 Sheet of Cream Pattern (AG041)
1 Sheet of Pink Pattern (AG044)
1 Pink Oval Frame (AG433)
Ivory Cardstock
Envelope, 6½" x 4¾"
Baby Girl Image
Foam Adhesive
Ivory Ribbon, ¼" wide
Hole Punch, ⅛"

Directions
Cut a 9" x 6¼" piece from the ivory cardstock. Score and fold in half to form a 4½" x 6¼" card. Cover the card with pink patterned paper.

Cut a 4" x 5¾" piece of the cream patterned paper and adhere to the pink patterned paper.

Punch out the oval frame and adhere to the cream patterned paper. Adhere a baby image to the oval frame.

Laser-print or handwrite "It's a Girl!" onto ivory cardstock. Punch a hole in the end and thread with the ivory ribbon. Tie in a loose knot as shown. Adhere to card front with bow.

Create a coordinating envelope liner with the pink patterned paper.

Apply glass finish to the four floral images, according to the directions, and allow to dry completely. Adhere in the four corners as shown. Adhere a baby boy image to the card.

Laser-print or handwrite "Its a Boy!" onto ivory cardstock. Punch a hole in the end and thread with the ivory ribbon. Tie in a loose knot as shown. Adhere to card front.

Create a coordinating envelope liner with the blue striped paper.

Its A Boy! Card
Materials
1 Sheet of Cream Pattern (AG041)
1 Sheet of Blue Pattern (AG045)
1 Sheet of Blue Stripes (AG022)
4 Flower Images
Ivory Cardstock
Envelope, 6½" x 4¾"
Baby Boy Image
Fold Art Papier Glass Finish
   (Plaid Enterprises 1777)
Foam Adhesive
Ivory Ribbon, ¼" wide
Hole Punch, ⅛"

Directions
Cut a 9" x 6¼" piece from the ivory cardstock. Score and fold in half to form a 4½" x 6 ¼" card. Cover the card with blue patterned paper.

Cut a 4" x 5¾" piece of the cream patterned paper and adhere to the blue patterned paper. Cut a 4" x 4¾" piece of the blue patterned paper and adhere it to the cream patterned paper. Top with a 4½" x 3" piece of blue striped paper.

Baby Announcement Card
Materials

1 Sheet of Blue Pattern (AG174)
1 Sheet of Blue Floral (AG178)
1 Sheet of Blue Bunnies (AG191)
1 Sheet of Red Pattern (AG193)
1 Bunnies Diecut (AG539)
Ivory Sheer Ribbon, 1" wide
Ivory Cardstock
Envelope, 6½" x 4¾"
Foam Adhesive
Hole Punch
Decorative-edged Scissors, Scallop

Directions

Cut ivory cardstock to 9" x 6¼". Score and fold in half to form a 4½" x 6¼" card. Trim away the top corners of the card to resemble a tag shape. Cover with a slightly smaller piece of the blue patterned paper.

Cut a 3¾" square of the blue floral paper, trim with the decorative scissors and adhere to the blue patterned paper. Cut a 3¼" square of the red patterned paper and adhere to the blue floral square. Cut a 2¾" square of the blue bunnies paper and adhere to the red patterned square.

Punch out the bunnies diecut. Adhere the layers to the card for a three-dimensional effect. Punch a hole at the top of the card. Thread the hole with the ivory sheer ribbon and finish with a loose knot.

Create a coordinating envelope liner with the red patterned paper.

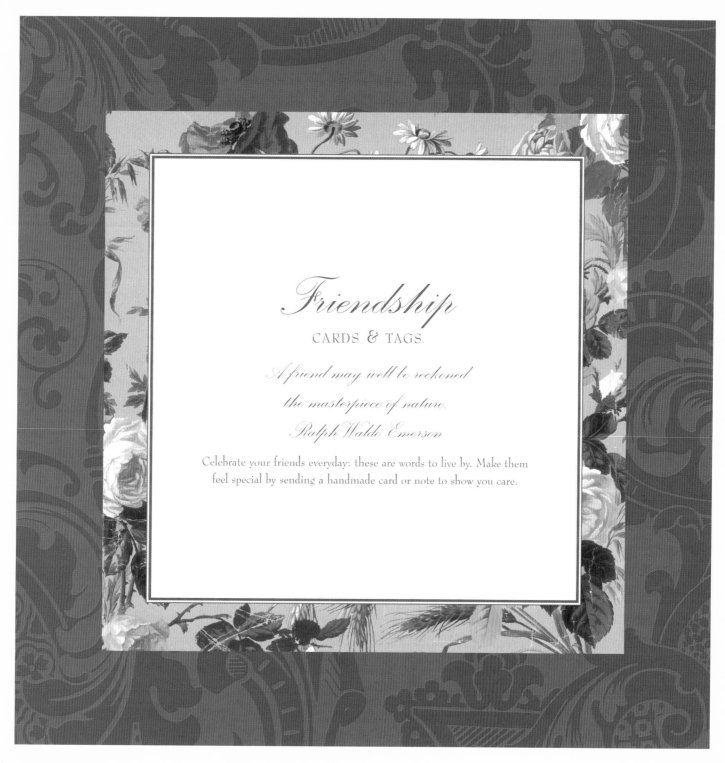

Friendship

CARDS & TAGS

A friend may well be reckoned

the masterpiece of nature.

Ralph Waldo Emerson

Celebrate your friends everyday: these are words to live by. Make them
feel special by sending a handmade card or note to show you care.

Tags can be very simple to make yet dramatic in results. The tag and embellishments punch out so you can make a tag in minutes.

Inspired by an awning, this pretty pocket
card conceals your greeting inside with
market stripes and decorative ribbon.

Tag art is a new phenomenon. Easy to make and highly decorative, tags are perfect for gifts, scrapbook pages, and cards.

MY FRIEND

FOR A
SPECIAL
FRIEND

Inspired by a wedding garter, this card has a
hidden pocket that conceals your well wishes.

the folded cardstock. Punch out the holes at the end of the tags and thread pink ribbon through. Finish by tying the ribbon into a loose knot as shown.

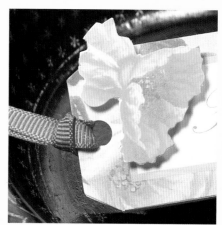

Friendship

CARDS & TAGS

Friends Forever Tag
Materials
2 Diecut Friendship Tags (AG534)
Ivory Cardstock
Pink Grosgrain Ribbon
Foam Adhesive

Directions

Punch out each of the die-cut friendship tags. Layer and adhere the flowers and butterfly piece on top of the tags.

On the ivory cardstock, trace the two tags side-by-side with the long ends touching. Cut out the ivory cardstock and fold in half. Adhere a tag to each side of the folded cardstock. One tag will be upside down.

Write your sentiment on the inside of

Best Friends Pocket Card
Materials

1 Sheet Floral Paper (AG147)
1 Sheet Pink Stripes (AG149)
1 Sheet Plum Pattern (AG154)
1 Diecut Friendship Tag (AG534)
Ivory Cardstock, 12" x 12"
Pink Grosgrain Ribbon
Decorative-edged Scissors, Scallop
Foam Adhesive

Directions

Cut the ivory cardstock to 12" x 4½".
Cover one side with the pink striped
paper. Cover the other side with the
floral paper. Score horizontally 2¼"
from the top, then again at 8½" from
the top.

Fold the top flap down. Trim the edge
with the scallop scissors. Fold the
bottom flap up and adhere the sides to
the back of the card to form a pocket.

Cut a 1" x 9½" strip of the plum
patterned paper. Wrap it around the card
as shown and adhere in the back. Adhere
a length of the pink ribbon on top of
this strip.

Cut a 4" x 5½" card from the ivory cardstock. Handwrite or laser-print the sentiment onto this card and place it into
the pocket.

Punch out the "Best Friends" diecut tag
and adhere to the top flap.

Cut a ¾" x 8" strip of the blue patterned paper. Mark and score across the paper at every ¼". Accordion-fold where scored and adhere this pencil-pleated strip in the back.

Cut a ¾" x 8" strip of the blue patterned paper. Mark and score across the paper at every ¼". Fold the first score forward and the next score backward, continuing across the strip to create a box-pleated strip. Adhere in the back.

Layer and adhere the die-cut blue roses to the tag for a three-dimensional effect.

Adhere both pleated strips on top of the red patterned paper as shown. Top with alternating ¾" squares of the blue/green floral and the pink patterned papers.

Handwrite or laser-print your sentiment onto ivory cardstock. Trim out and adhere to the tag.

Pleated Tag
Materials

1 Sheet of Red Pattern (AG157)
1 Sheet of Pink Pattern (AG159)
1 Sheet Green Floral (AG170)
1 Sheet of Blue/Green Floral (AG171)
1 Sheet of Blue Pattern (AG174)
1 Sheet of Green Pattern (AG185)
1 Blue Roses Floral Diecut (AG536)
Ivory Cardstock
Decorative-edged Scissors, Scallop
Blue Wire-edged Ribbon
Hole Punch
Foam adhesive

Directions

Cut a 3" x 6" tag from the ivory cardstock. Cover with the green patterned paper. Cut a 1½" x 3" piece of the green floral paper and adhere to bottom of the tag.

Cut a 2" x 3" piece of the red patterned paper. Trim each 3" side with the scallop scissors and adhere to the tag where the green floral paper meets the green paterned paper.

Pleated Pocket Card
Materials
1 Sheet of Blue Pattern (AG174)
1 Sheet of Red Solid (AG157)
1 Sheet of Green Pattern (AG172)
Ivory Cardstock
Foam Adhesive
Decorative-edged Scissors, Zigzag
Hole Punch

Directions
Cut a 7" x 9" piece from ivory cardstock. Cover each side with the blue patterned paper. Score and fold 5" from the top. Measure ½" in from each side, score and fold to form flaps. Cut away excess cardstock. Adhere flaps in place.

Cut a 2" x 12" strip of the green patterned paper. Mark and score across the paper at every ¼". Fold the first score forward and the next score backward, continuing across the strip to create a box-pleated strip. Adhere pleats in place in the back of the strip. Adhere across the center of the card as shown.

Cut a 1" x 6" strip from the red patterned paper with the zigzag scissors. Adhere in the center of the green pleated strip.

Cut a ¾" x 12" strip of the blue patterned paper. Mark and score across the paper at every ¼". Fold the first score forward and the next score backward, continuing across the strip to create a box-pleated strip. Adhere pleats in place in the back of the strip. Adhere to the red strip.

Handwrite or laser-print your sentiment onto ivory cardstock and trim into a 2" square. Mat with a slightly larger piece of the red patterned paper. Cut edges with the zigzag scissors and adhere to the pleated strip.

Cut a 5½" x 4½" piece from ivory cardstock. Adhere a ⅛" strip of red paper, cut with the zigzag scissors, to the top of the card. Punch a hole in the top-left corner of the card and finish with a loose knot of blue ribbon.

Holiday

CARDS & TAGS

May Peace be your gift at Christmas and

your blessing all year through!

Author Unknown

Making my own Christmas cards has been a tradition in my
family ever since I can remember. There's nothing like getting together
with family and friends to make the following glorious creations.

No need to force this Amaryllis bulb early, it's in full bloom from Thanksgiving through Christmas!

This bold, graphic Poinsettia diecut is the star of the show on this handmade card. The card unfolds in the center like a gate to reveal your greeting.

The "Joy" of scrapbooking comes to life using this handmade tag as the title for the page.

By layering multiple diecuts, you can form a beautiful wreath to frame that special holiday photo.

Happy Holidays

These tags do double duty as package embellishments and works of art.

Striped papers, like the stripes on a candy cane,
make scrapbook pages look good enough to eat.
The candy cane tag is a yummy treat!

Use this tag year after year to adorn those special presents that need an extraordinary touch.

FOR

Mother

FROM

Anna

Just like the belt that Santa wears, the velvet ribbon and buckle are the accessories that make the outfit.

Merry Christmas

This cards displays the beauty and abundance that is Thanksgiving. Giving thanks has never been easier.

HAPPY *Thanksgiving*

Holiday

CARDS & TAGS

Amaryllis Wishes Card
Materials

1 Sheet of Green Pattern (AG1051)
1 Sheet of Red Solid (AG017)
1 Sheet of Red Pattern (AG162)
1 Amaryllis Floral Diecut (AG527)
Ivory Bow (RC211)
Ivory Cardstock
Envelope, 4¾" x 6½"
Decorative-edged Scissors, Scallop
Foam Adhesive

Directions

Cut ivory cardstock to 6" x 9". Score and fold in half to form a 4½" x 6" card. Cover the card with the red solid paper.

Tear a 5½" x 4" rectangle from the green patterned paper. Center and adhere to the card front.

Layer and adhere the die-cut amaryllis flowers to the green patterned paper for a three-dimensional effect.

Handwrite or laser-print the sentiment onto ivory cardstock. Trim out a tag shape with the scallop scissors.

Adhere the tag and the small ivory bow to the floral layer as shown.

Create a coordinating envelope liner with the red patterned paper.

Cut two 2" x 4½" pieces from the green patterned paper. Score and fold in half vertically. On one, trim the left edge with the ripple scissors. On the other, trim the right edge with the ripple scissors.

Adhere these strips onto each side of the gatefold card at the fold.

Create a coordinating envelope liner with the green patterned paper.

Poinsettia Gatefold Card
Materials
1 Sheet of Holly Floral (AG105)
1 Sheet of Poinsettia Floral (AG106)
1 Sheet of Green Pattern (AG051)
1 Sheet of Red Stripes (AG095)
1 Poinsettia Floral Diecut (AG529)
Ivory Cardstock, 12" x 12"
Envelope, 6½" x 4¾"
Decorative-edged Scissors, Ripple

Directions
Cut ivory cardstock to 12" x 4½". Score and fold toward the center at 3" and 9" to form a gatefold card.

Cover the outside of the card with the holly floral paper. Cover the inside with the poinsettia floral paper.

Cut a ½" x 12" stripe from the red striped paper. Wrap around the card and adhere in the center.

Joy Scrapbook Page & Tag

Materials
1 Sheet of Red Floral (AG024)
1 Sheet of Red Pattern (AG082)
1 Sheet of Gold Texture Pattern
   (AG179)
1 Sheet of Gold Damask (AG802)
1 Red Floral Diecut (AG517)
Gold Alphabet Stickers (AG634)
Ivory Cardstock
Decorative-edged Scissors, Zigzag
4 Ivory Buttons, ¾"
Gold Satin Bow
Gold Satin Ribbon, ¼" wide
Foam Adhesive

Directions
Cut four 1" x 11" strips of the red floral paper. Mat each with a ⅛" border of the red patterned paper and adhere around the edges of a sheet of gold patterned paper.

Cut four 1¼" squares of the second gold patterned paper. Mat each with a ⅛" border of the red patterned paper and adhere to the corners of the red floral border. Top each with a button that has been tied with the ¼"-wide gold ribbon.

Mat photo with a 1" border of the red

floral, then with a ⅛" border of the red patterned paper, then with a ¼" border of the gold patterned paper. Adhere to page.

Layer and adhere the die-cut flowers to the page for a three-dimensional effect.

For the tag, cut a 2½" x 5" tag shape from the gold patterned paper, using the zigzag scissors. Decorate with the red patterned and floral papers. Finish with a 3" x 1" piece of ivory cardstock on top. Spell "Joy" with the stickers and finish with the gold bow.

Handwrite or laser-print your holiday sentiment onto ivory cardstock. Trim out and adhere to the card. Finish with

a red bow adhered to the top of the card. Create a coordinating envelope liner with the gold patterned paper.

Wreath Frame Photo Card
Materials
1 Sheet of Red Floral (AG024)
1 Sheet of Gold Pattern (AG027)
1 Sheet of Red Pattern (AG082)
1 Sheet of Gold Pattern (AG802)
3 Red Floral Diecuts (AG517)
Ivory Cardstock
Envelope, 7¼" x 5¼"
Red Ribbon
Foam Adhesive

Directions
Cut ivory cardstock to 10" x 7". Score and fold in half to form a 5" x 7" card. Cover the card with the red patterned paper. Trim a 4¾" x 6¾" piece of the gold patterned paper and adhere to the front of the card.

For the frame, adhere the photo to the center of the card. Decoratively layer and adhere the die-cut flowers around the photo for a three-dimensional "wreath" frame.

Christmas Tags
Materials

1 Sheet of Gold Pattern (AG003)
1 Sheet of Dark Green Pattern
   (AG163)
1 Sheet of Gold Pattern (AG802)
1 Sheet of Green Stripes (AG832)
1 Sheet of Gold Stripes (AG834)
1 Holly Floral Diecut (AG528)
Ivory Cardstock
Foam Adhesive
Gold Satin Ribbon
Red Ribbon
Christmas Tree Image
Hole Punch

Directions

Cut two 2½" x 4¼" tags from ivory cardstock. For the holly tag, cover the front with gold patterned paper. Cut a 1½" x 4¼" strip of the gold striped paper and adhere to the center of the gold patterned paper.

Cut a ½" x 4¼" strip of the dark green patterned paper and adhere to the center of the gold striped strip.

Layer and adhere the die-cut holly to the center of the tags for a three-dimensional effect. Punch a hole at the top and thread with the red ribbon. Finish with a loose knot.

For the Christmas tree tag, cover the front with green patterned paper. Cut a 1½" x 4¼" strip of the green striped paper and adhere to the center of the green patterned paper.

Cut a 2" x 3½" piece of the gold patterned paper and adhere it to the center of the tag.

Adhere the Christmas tree image to the center of the tag. Punch a hole at the top of the tag and thread with the gold satin ribbon. Finish with a loose knot.

ivory cardstock, trimmed with the scallop scissors, a ¼" x 11" piece of red striped paper, a 1" x 11" piece of green striped paper, a 2" x 11" piece of holly paper, a 1½" x 11" piece of red striped paper, a 2" x 11" piece of candy cane paper, a 1" x 11" piece of green striped paper, and a 1¾" piece of holly paper.

Punch out the diecut frame and mat the photo. Adhere to the page as shown. Cut out three bows from the candy cane paper. Adhere the bows to the frame.

Cut several ¼" stripes from the red striped paper. Stamp sentiment with crimson ink onto ivory cardstock and trim to 5" x 1½". Edge with the red stripes, mitering the corners. Adhere to the page.

Create the tag as described on page 109, using the green patterned paper and the red striped paper. Cut out a candy cane from the candy cane paper to embellish. Finish with the red gingham ribbon and adhere to the page.

Candy Cane Christmas Page Materials
1 Sheet of Red Pattern (AG162)
1 Sheet of Green Pattern (AG163)
2 Sheets of Candy Cane (AG831)
1 Sheet of Holly Floral (AG821)
1 Sheet Green Stripes (AG832)
1 Sheet Red Stripes (AG833)
1 Diecut 4-in-1 Frame (AG441)
Anna Griffin Holiday Sentiment Stamp
  (Plaid Enterprises 580G06)
Anna Griffin Crimson Inkpad
  (Plaid Enterprises 19ABG)
Ivory Cardstock, 12" x 12"

Foam Adhesive
Red Gingham Ribbon
Decorative-edged Scissors, Scallop

Directions
Trim red patterned paper to an 11½" square and adhere to the center of the green patterned paper.

For the next layer, trim the following papers and adhere them, slightly overlapping, from left to right, on top of the red patterned paper: a 1½" x 11" piece of candy cane paper, a ½" x 11" piece of

Brass Frame Tag
Materials

1 Sheet of Green Pattern (AG163)
1 Sheet of Red Pattern (AG195)
1 Holly Floral Diecut (AG528)
Anna Griffin Gift Tags & Greetings
    Stamp Set (Plaid Enterprises, 2449R)
Anna Griffin Gold Inkpad,
    (Plaid Enterprises 19AGL)
Anna Griffin Brass Frame Embellishment
    (Plaid Enterprises 79TFF)
Red Velvet Ribbon
Ivory Cardstock
Foam Adhesive

Directions

Cut ivory cardstock to 3¼" x 4¾". Cut green patterned paper to 3¼" x 4¾" and cut a 1¾" x 3¼" window in the center.

Handwrite or laser-print your names onto the cardstock. Stamp "For" and "From" with gold ink. Adhere the green paper frame on top of the cardstock.

Cut two ½" x 3" and two ½" x 4½" strips of the red patterned paper. Adhere around the green frame as shown, mitering the corners.

Adhere the brass frame embellishment to the red and green frame. Adhere the holly pieces to the corners of the frame.

Finish with a loop of red velvet ribbon at the top of the tag.

Wrap the red ribbon across the green patterned strip and adhere in place. Laser-print or handwrite the sentiment onto ivory cardstock. Trim out and adhere to the back of the brass frame. Adhere the frame to the red ribbon.

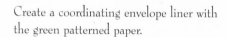

Create a coordinating envelope liner with the green patterned paper.

Santa's Belt Card
Materials
1 Sheet of Green Pattern (AG163)
1 Sheet of Red Pattern (AG195)
Anna Griffin Brass Frame Embellishment
   (Plaid Enterprises 79TLF)
Ivory Cardstock
Envelope, 5¾" x 4¼"
Santa Claus Image
Red Velvet Ribbon
Decorative-edged Scissors, Zigzag
Foam Adhesive

Directions
Cut ivory cardstock to 9" x 5½". Score and fold in half to form a 4½" x 5½" card. Cover the card with the red patterned paper.

Adhere the Santa Claus image to the front of the card. Cut a 1¾" x 4½" strip of the green patterned paper. Trim the top edge with the zigzag scissors and adhere to the bottom of the card.

Thanksgiving Card
Materials

1 Sheet of Red Pattern (AG157)
2 sheets of Floral (AG116)
1 Sheet Gold Journal Blocks (AG241)
Anna Griffin Sentiment Stamp Set
   (Plaid Enterprises 48100)
Foam Adhesive
Gold Satin Ribbon, ¼" wide
Hole Punch, ⅛"

Directions

Adhere the red patterned paper to the floral paper, back to back.

With the red pattern facing up, measure a 6" square in the center of the sheet, 3" in from each side. Score and fold the outline of this square. Cut away a 2½" circle from each side of the four flaps and fold up the flaps.

Cut out the square journaling block and adhere to the front of the top flap. Cut out several flowers from the floral paper and adhere to the journaling block as shown.

Stamp the sentiment onto a small journaling block with black ink. Cut out in the shape of a tag and punch a hole in the top. Thread the hole with the gold satin ribbon and finish with a loose knot. Adhere tag to the front of the card.

113

With Love

CARDS & TAGS

*Life's greatest happiness is to be
convinced we are loved.*

Victor Hugo

Need a little inspiration for expressing your deepest feelings?
Make a card, make a book, make a tag:
they all will say "I love you" in style.

Pretty in pink, this elaborately wrapped gatefold card is a project worth making.

Why I Love You

This little book is full of sentimental phrases bound together as a gift of love.

Love birds, vellum, and pleated paper combine to make an elegant card fit for a queen.

This tag is unique because I've used alphabet stickers and then cut them away with a craft knife.

HOLLEY & JEFF
AUGUST 25, 2001

LOVE

Cut two, 1" x 7" strips of the pink solid paper and trim one edge of each with the scallop scissors. Adhere to the front of the card, along the gatefold edges as shown.

Cut two, 4" squares from the ivory cardstock, using scallop scissors. Adhere a 3½" square of pink patterned paper to each one.

Fold the squares behind the gatefold flaps so that the two squares align to form a diamond shape on the front of the card as shown. Adhere in place.

Cut a hole on each side of the diamond shape. Wrap the ivory ribbon around the card and thread an end into each hole. Tie ribbon into a bow.

Handwrite or laser-print your sentiment onto ivory cardstock and trim out in a small tag shape with the mini-scallop scissors. Adhere to the card.

With Love

CARDS & TAGS

With Love Gatefold Card
Materials
1 Sheet Pink Pattern (AG044)
1 Sheet Pink Floral (AG054)
1 Sheet Pink Solid (AG015)
Ivory Cardstock, 12" x 12"
Ivory Ribbon

Foam Adhesive
Decorative-edged Scissors, Scallop
Decorative-edged Scissors, Mini Scallop

Directions
Cut cardstock to 10" x 7". Cover with the pink patterned paper. Score 2½" from the left side and again at 7½" from the left side. Fold flaps up to create a gatefold card.

Why I Love You Booklet Card
Materials
1 Sheet Floral (AG012)
1 Sheet Pink Pattern (AG085)
Ivory Cardstock
Embossed Ivory Cardstock
Pink Ribbon
Decorative-edged Scissors, Zigzag

Directions
Cut two 3" x 4" pieces of the embossed ivory cardstock. Cut a 3¼" x 4" piece of the floral paper. Score every ¼" and accordion-fold to form the spine of the booklet.

Adhere one ivory cardstock piece to the first ¼" flap of the accordion-folded piece. Adhere the second ivory cardstock piece to the last ¼" flap of the accordion-folded piece.

Cut five 2½" x 3¾" pieces of ivory cardstock for the booklet pages. Handwrite your sentiments onto these pieces and adhere each one to a flap in the accordion-folded spine.

Wrap a length of pink ribbon around the booklet, allowing enough extra ribbon to tie a bow. Adhere the ribbon in place around the booklet.

Cut a 1¾" x 2¾" piece from the ivory cardstock. Handwrite or laser-print cover sentiment onto this card.

Mat with a slightly larger piece of the pink patterned paper and trim with the zigzag scissors. Mat with a slightly larger piece of the floral paper and adhere to the front of the card, on top of the ribbon. Finish by tying the ribbon into a bow.

forward, continuing across the strips. Adhere the pleats in the back.

Adhere the pleated strips to the edges of the card. Miter the corners. Cut a 5½" x 3½" piece of the pink patterned paper and adhere to the center of the card, slightly overlapping the pleated edges.

Layer and adhere the die-cut floral on to the pink patterned paper for a three-dimensional effect.

Handwrite or laser-print your sentiment onto vellum. Trim to a 4½" x 3" piece and adhere to the back of the die-cut floral as shown. Adhere to the card over the pink paper.

Accent with the gold bow. Create a coordinating envelope liner with the pink patterned paper.

Pleated Love Card
Materials

1 Sheet of Green Pattern (AG131)
1 Sheet of Pink Pattern (AG168)
1 Floral Diecut (AG523)
Gold Bow (RC212)
Vellum
Ivory Cardstock
Envelope, 7¼" x 5¼"
Foam Adhesive

Directions

Cut a 10" x 7" piece of the ivory cardstock. Score and fold in half to form a 5" x 7" card. Cut a 1½" x 3" piece of the green floral paper and adhere to the bottom of the tag.

Cut a 4" x 12" piece of the green patterned paper. Mark and score across the 12" length of the paper at every ¼". Trim into four, 1" x 12" strips. Fold the strips into box pleats by folding the first score backward and the next score

Love Scrapbook Page & Tag
Materials
1 Sheet of Floral (AG012)
3 Sheets of Green Pattern (AG043)
2 Sheets of Pink Pattern (AG082)
Alphabet Stickers (AG630)
Embossed Ivory Cardstock
Ivory Cardstock
Foam Adhesive
Green Satin Ribbon
Hole Punch

Directions
Cut one sheet of the pink patterned to an 11¼" square. Adhere to one sheet of green patterned paper. Cut the floral paper to a 10" square and adhere to the pink patterned paper.

Cut four 1" x 11" strips of embossed cardstock. Adhere them around the edges of the floral paper, leaving only the pink patterned paper edge exposed. Miter the corners. Mat photo with a slightly

larger piece of pink patterned paper. Mat this with a slightly larger piece of green patterned and mat again with a slightly larger piece of pink patterned paper. Adhere to the center of the page.

For the tag, cut a 5½" x 2½" tag shape from the second sheet of green patterned paper. Mat with a slightly larger piece of pink patterned paper. Cut out two 3½" x 1½" pieces of ivory cardstock.

Spell out "Love" with the alphabet stickers on one of the cardstock pieces. Carefully trim out the letters from the cardstock. Adhere the die-cut piece to the second piece of cardstock, then adhere to the front of the tag. Punch a

hole at the end of the tag. Tie a loose knot with the green satin ribbon.

Cut out the flowers from the remaining green patterned paper. Decoratively adhere the flowers around the photo and onto the. Adhere the tag to the page.

Handwrite or laser-print your sentiment onto ivory cardstock and adhere among the cut flowers.

Materials & Techniques

CARDS & TAGS

*True art is characterized by an
irresistible urge in the creative artist.*
Albert Einstein

Templates supporting each project, if suggested, will be found in the next
section of this book. In the materials lists, the papers, motifs, and diecuts are
suggestions only. If the exact Anna Griffin products are desired, refer to the
catalog numbers indicated in parentheses after the item's description.

Materials

You can create extraordinary cards and tags with just a few simple materials. It is important that your supplies be acid-free and of archival quality. You may have other tools or materials that make these projects easier to construct—feel free to use them!

Basic Materials

You'll also need these basic materials for paper crafting:

- A **craft knife** for making clean straight cuts in papers and for cutting out intricate designs.

- A self-healing **cutting mat** for cutting with a craft knife.

- A **metal ruler** to use as a straightedge for cutting.

- A **triangle** for angled cuts.

- A pair of **scissors** for trimming papers and cutting out motifs for decoupage or embellishments.

- A soft-lead **pencil** for lightly marking measurements.

- A **stylus** or **bone folder** to aid in scoring and folding.

Decorative Paper

You can use a variety of papers for card and tag crafting. Many of the projects in this book feature Anna Griffin Decorative Papers that may be used alone or mixed together with coordinating solid or stamped papers.

Cards, Tags & Envelopes

You can create your own card surfaces, tags and envelopes using cardstock and paper, or you may choose to buy premade surfaces, available at many craft stores.

Ribbon

Create your own bows, trims, and embellishments with ribbon. It is the perfect finishing touch for any paper-crafting project.

Punches

Decorative paper punches add intricate designs quickly and easily to your projects. Choose from corner designs, borders and motifs. A hole punch is also handy for punching holes in tags and for threading ribbon.

Decorative-edged Scissors

Many projects in the book use decorative-edged scissors to create a diecut effect. These scissors come in a variety of designs such as scallop, deckle, and others. Decorative-edged scissors are widely available where craft products are found.

Adhesives

There are lots of wonderful adhesives available for crafting. Double-sided tape is used in many instances for adhering on cutouts and borders. Be sure to choose acid-free, archival-quality adhesives.

Foam adhesive tape or dots are a great way to add dimension to a project. When placed under cut-out paper motifs, they raise the design above the surface and give a dimension to the design.

Embellishments

There are hundreds of embellishments for card and tag making, available at your local craft store. Be creative and make your own with your paper scraps or found objects. Cut out flowers or other motifs from printed papers, then layer and adhere them with foam tape to add dimension to your projects.

Techniques

Sometimes, a little help goes a long way. From paper pleating to tying the perfect bow, learning a few simple techniques can add dramatic impact to your paper-crafting projects.

Using a Rubber Stamp

It is best to stamp on a flat padded surface such as a magazine or a stack of paper. This will ensure an even impression of the entire image. Start with a clean stamp. Practice on scrap paper before you stamp your project.

1. Gently tap the rubber side of the stamp on the pigment ink pad, covering the stamp completely with ink.

2. Press the stamp carefully but firmly on your paper or cardstock.

3. To prevent smearing, lift the rubber stamp straight up.

Tips:

- Make certain to apply even pressure to the stamp; the larger the stamp, the more pressure is required for a good impression.

- Don't rock the stamp! Rocking may produce back-printing from extra ink on the outside edges.

Cleaning Stamps

Always clean your stamp when changing ink colors. Use a stamp cleaner or soap and water to remove the ink, then blot the stamp until dry on a paper towel.

Stamping with Two Colors

You can create dramatic, two-color stamping effects, using just one stamp. To do this, stamp one color at a time.

1. Cover the portion of the stamp you want to be the second color with a piece of paper.

2. Ink your stamp with the first ink color and stamp the image. Clean the stamp.

3. Repeat the process for the remaining portion of the stamp and the second ink color, carefully aligning the stamped images.

Heat Embossing

Heat embossing can add texture to stamp art. Use embossing powder and an embossing heat tool to produce a shiny raised finish.

1. Stamp the design with ink.

2. Before the ink dries, pour embossing powder generously over the stamped image. Tap off any excess powder.

3. Heat the image for about 10 seconds with an embossing heat tool. You will see the powder melt and turn into a shiny raised image.

Using a Craft Knife

Use a craft knife for precision cutting on your craft projects. For precise straight cuts, work on a cutting mat, hold the knife like a pencil, and drag it toward you, following the edge of a metal ruler.

Tips:

- Always cut toward your body to maintain control over the knife.

- A good, sharp blade is essential for neat edges, so change the blade frequently.

- Always keep knives and blades out of the reach of children.

Paper Punching

Paper punching is a great way to make intricate cuts in paper quickly and easily.

1. Place the punch on a firm surface.

2. Slide the paper or cardstock between the punch blades.

3. Press down on the top of the punch until the paper pops out.

Tips:

- For best results, lubricate the punch by punching a piece of waxed paper.

- To sharpen and clean your punch, punch through aluminum foil.

- To position a punch exactly, turn the punch over to align.

Embossing with Brass Stencils

Brass stencils can create elegant, embossed, dimensional designs on paper quickly and easily.

1. Position the stencil on a light box or light source. Secure the cardstock face down on the stencil. For best results, use a low tack adhesive.

2. Rub waxed paper over the paper surface to make it pliable.

3. Trace over the stencil design with a stylus or embossing tool, applying pressure along the edges of the cut-out areas of the stencil. Repeat, if necessary.

4. When all areas are embossed, remove the stencil and turn the card over.

Scoring & Folding

Scoring paper and cardstock makes it much easier to fold. To make crisp folds, you will need a straightedge, a stylus, and a bone folder.

1. Place the straightedge where you want the fold to be. Score the line with the stylus. You could also use a butter knife or an empty ballpoint pen to score.

2. Fold the card along the scored line. Run the bone folder or a burnisher along the fold to make it crisp.

Pencil Pleating

Pencil pleating is a paper-folding technique that creates even pleats, or folds, in one direction.

1. Using a ruler and a pencil, measure and make light pencil marks on the back of the paper at ⅝" and ⅞" increments along top and bottom of areas to be pleated.

2. Using a straightedge and a stylus, score the lines, placing the straightedge at the marks.

3. Fold back and forth, making an accordion fold.

Mitering Corners

Mitering joins two strips of paper together, creating a 45-degree diagonal line at the right-angle corner where the two strips meet. This is the technique used to make paper frames. To start, cut the strips of paper the width and length needed to create the frame.

1. Glue the strips together at a right angle, overlapping the ends. Use repositionable glue, or work quickly to create the miter before the glue completely dries.

2. Position a straightedge diagonally across the corner. With a craft knife, cut through both pieces from the inside corner to the outside corner.

3. Remove the triangles of paper on the top and bottom where the strips overlap to reveal a mitered corner.

Making an Envelope

Ready to test your math skills? You can make envelopes to fit any size card. Use glue or double-sided tape to seal the top flap of the envelope after you insert the card.

1. Measure your card and add ½" to the height and width. (This is your base size.)

2. Add a bottom flap that is three-quarters of the base height.

3. Add a top flap that is one-fourth of the base height plus 1".

4. Add side flaps that are one-half the base width plus ⅛".

5. Taper all flaps slightly as shown on the Envelope template below.

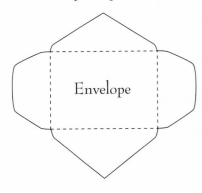

Envelope

6. Mark the fold lines and score, using a metal ruler and a bone folder or an embossing tool.

7. Fold in the side flaps. Apply glue to the edges of the bottom flap and fold over the side flaps. Fold down the top flap.

Making an Envelope Liner

It's easy to make a custom decorative envelope liner. The liner should fit just below the glue line of the envelope.

1. Cut a piece of paper just slightly smaller than the size of the open envelope to use as a pattern. Check the fit.

Cut

2. Trace around the pattern on the liner paper. Cut out. (It's best to use a straightedge and a craft knife.)

3. Decorate the liner to match the card. Use coordinating stamps and ink colors or decorative paper.

Decorate

4. Slide the liner into the envelope to check the fit and the look.

5. Remove the liner. Add adhesive to the top back edge and replace inside the envelope, pressing to adhere to the flap.

Adhere

Making Tags

There are many styles and colors of tags available at your local craft shop, but it's easy to make your own. Simply trace a Tag template onto cardstock and cut out. Punch a hole at the top to hang with ribbon or string. Decorate.

Tag

Tying a Bow

Create the perfect finishing touch with the the perfect bow:

1. Create ribbon loop and hold it in your left hand with your thumb, with the loop facing the ceiling.

2. With the shorter end in front, pointing toward your wrist, place the long end of the ribbon over the back, then up and over your hand.

3. Push a loop from the long end behind the first loop and through itself.

4. Pull left- and right-side loops tightly while holding down the streamers to create a symmetrical bow.

5. Adjust streamers and pull bow taut to finish. Trim the ends.

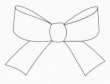

Tying a Square Knot

1. Wrap ribbon in place around card or project. Cross right end over left, push under the left side, and pull up.

2. Cross top end over bottom end. Push up through loop.

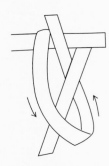

3. Pull the ribbon ends taught and trim away excess.

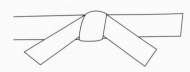

Tying a Threaded Knot

1. Punch two holes about ¼" apart on your card or surface. Cut a length of ribbon.

2. Thread each end of the ribbon down through separate holes on the front side.

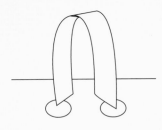

3. Cross ribbons in the back and feed the ribbon ends back through the front of the card.

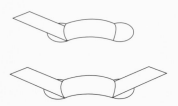

4. Pull the ends taut and trim.

Dovetailing

Dovetailing is a decorative way to finish a bow or knotted ribbon. After tying the bow or knot, fold the ends of the ribbon in half horizontally. Trim folded ribbon at an angle, approximately 1" in from the end. Unfold for the dovetail effect.

Templates

Scallop Tag
Pages 29, 54, 65, 105

Birthday Tag
Page 28

Floral Frame Birthday Tag
Page 31

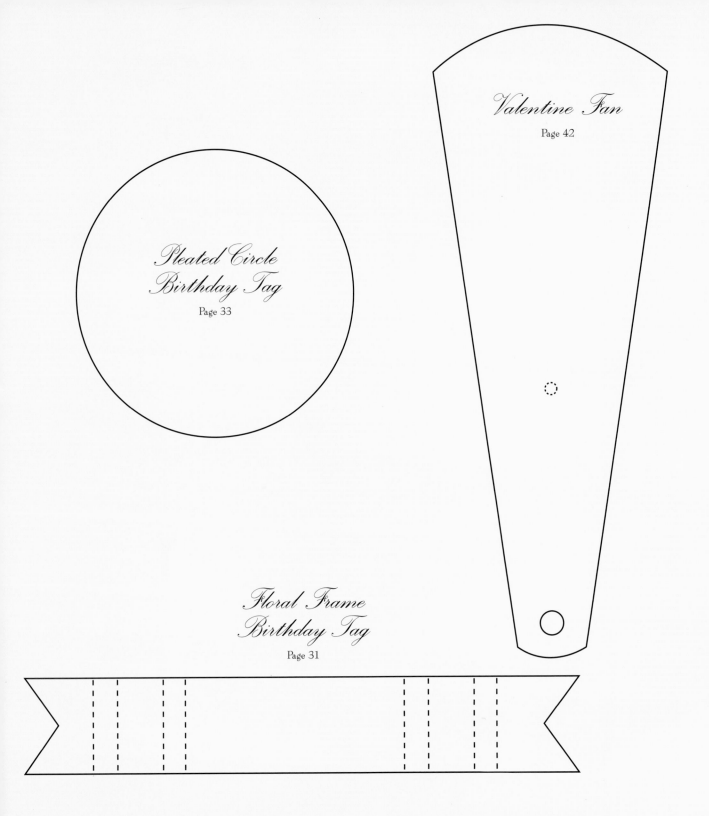

Pleated Circle
Birthday Tag
Page 33

Valentine Fan
Page 42

Floral Frame
Birthday Tag
Page 31

133

Be Mine
Valentine

Small Heart

Page 40

Be Mine
Valentine

Large Heart

Page 40

Woven Heart
Valentine

Large Heart

Page 43

Woven Heart
Valentine

Small Heart

Page 43

Flowers & Bows Tag

Large & Small Tags

Page 53

Floral Tag

Page 51

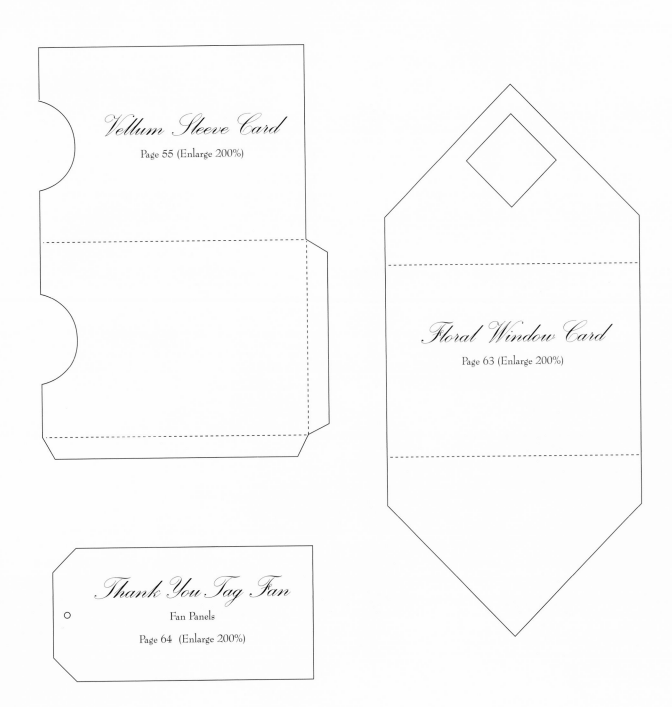

Vellum Sleeve Card

Page 55 (Enlarge 200%)

Floral Window Card

Page 63 (Enlarge 200%)

Thank You Tag Fan

Fan Panels

Page 64 (Enlarge 200%)

Bride & Groom Tag

Page 77

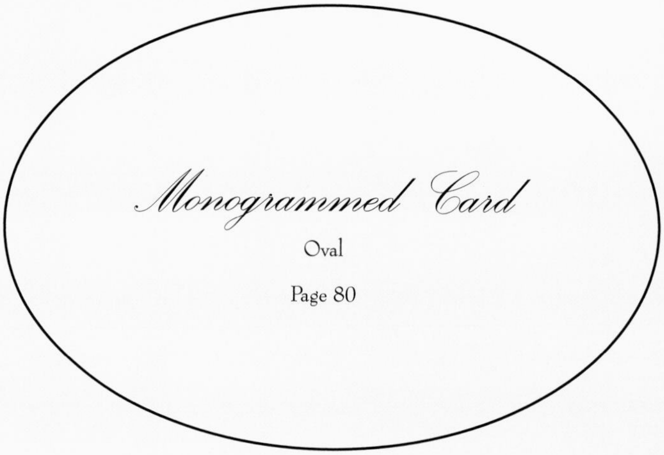

Monogrammed Card

Oval

Page 80

Congratulations Sleeve

Page 78 (Enlarge 200%)

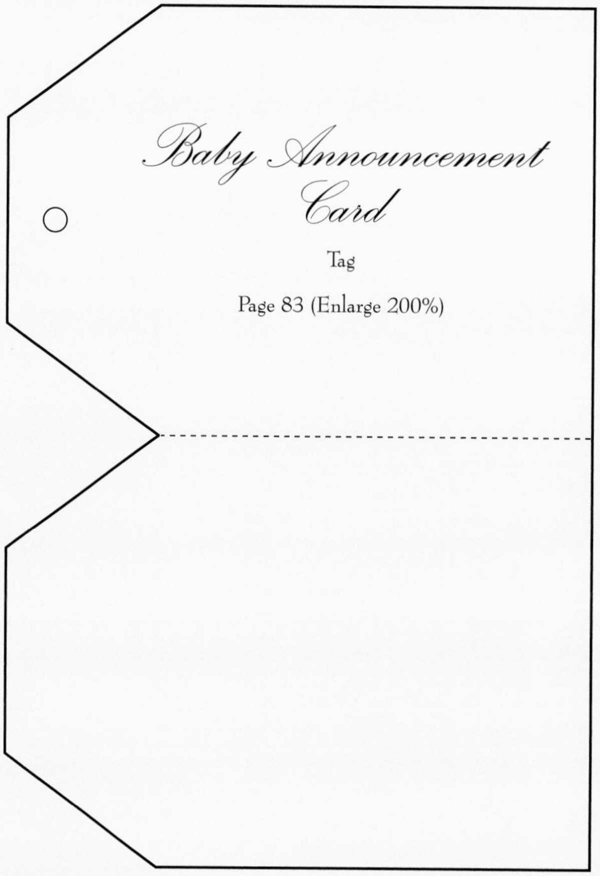

Baby Announcement Card

Tag

Page 83 (Enlarge 200%)

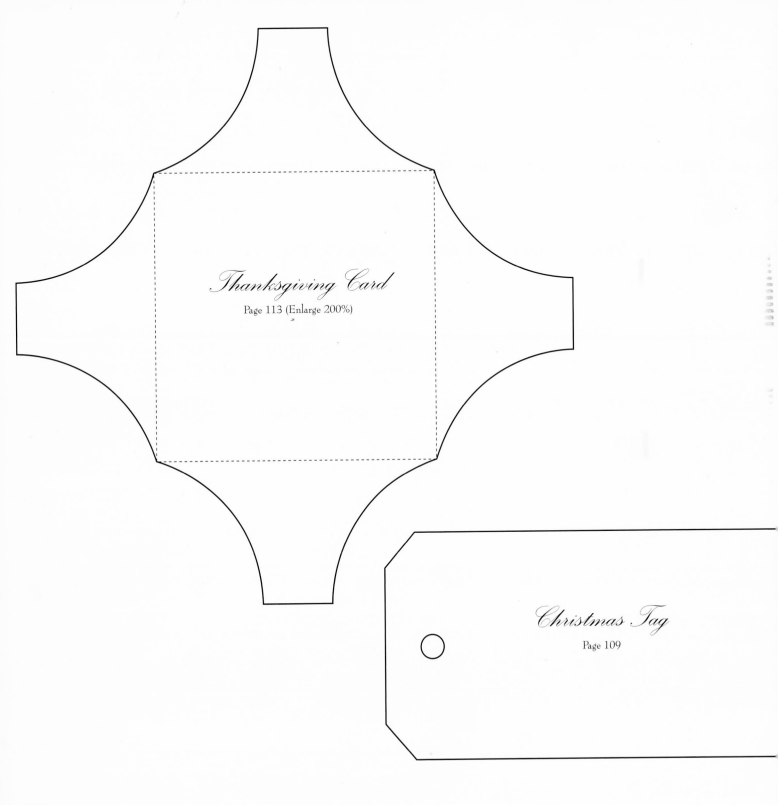

Thanksgiving Card
Page 113 (Enlarge 200%)

Christmas Tag
Page 109

Acknowledgments

Where would we be without those truly special people in our lives?

I know that I wouldn't be where I am without the strength and support of Tracey Flammer. I wouldn't look good or laugh without Holley Silirie. I wouldn't make my creative deadlines without Catherine Wingfield, Debby Schuh, and Jenna Beegle; and I wouldn't be here at all if it were not for my wonderful parents, Sallie and Charles. Thank you all, from the bottom of my heart for all you have given me!

Glossary

Accordion Fold - A fold like the bellows of an accordion, folds forward then backward, in repeat.

Acid-free - Refers to archival quality paper used for important records, scrapbooking, and storing photographs.

Archival - Having a neutral or slightly alkaline pH to last over time without decomposing; suitable for archiving.

Binding - The process of stitching or permanently adhering together a book.

Bone Folder - An instrument, used for scoring, folding or embossing paper.

Cartouche - An ornate or ornamental frame.

Chalking - A technique of coloring or aging paper by rubbing with chalk.

Chipboard - A thick cardboard available at art supply and craft stores.

Craft Knife - A knife with removable blade, commonly used for paper crafting, that makes precision cuts. Available at art supply and craft stores.

Cutting Mat - A self-healing mat used for cutting with a craft knife to protect the surface below. Available at art supply and craft stores.

Damask - Refers to a fabric of silk, wool, linen or cotton, with a distinct pattern formed by the weave.

Debossing - The process of making designs or patterns in negative relief on paper. The opposite of *Embossing*.

Decorative-edged Scissors - Scissors that cut with a flared edge rather than a straight edge. Available in many designs at art supply and craft stores.

Decorative Paper - Printed or textured paper used for crafting.

Decoupage - The art of decorating surfaces by applying paper cutouts and then coating with several layers of finish.

Diecut - To cut out around the edges of a print.

Dovetail - A notched end resembling a Dove's tail.

Dry Embossing - See "Embossing"

Embossing - The process of making designs or patterns in relief on paper.

Embossing Stylus - See *Stylus*

Eyelet - See *Grommet*

Foam Adhesive - A raised adhesive for adding dimension to crafts. Available at art supply and craft stores.

Grommet - A small, metal eyelet used to fasten papers.

Heat Embossing - A technique to simulate embossing using embossing powder and a heat source.

Journaling - The written story on a scrapbook page.

Light-box - A light source used for viewing slides or transparencies; In paper crafting, used for stenciling onto paper.

M

Metal Ruler - A straightedged strip made of steel, for drawing straight lines and measuring lengths.

Miter - The edge of a piece of paper that has been beveled to meet with a smooth 45-degree joint.

Monogram - A symbol of a name or names, consisting typically of a letter or several letters together.

Motif - A design or a thematic element.

P

Paper Punching - In paper crafting, to remove paper in designs or patterns, by using a punch tool.

Pigment Ink - Refers to ink used in rubber stamping with a thick consistency and rich color. Pigment inks will not dry on glossy surfaces.

Pleating - In paper crafting, to resemble a fold in cloth made by doubling material over on itself.

Q

Quilt - In paper crafts this refers to attaching or covering with lines or patterns like those used in sewn quilts.

R

Rubber Stamp - A stamp made of rubber used with an inkpad to make imprints and reproduce artwork.

S

Scoring Paper - A technique in paper crafting of preping paper fibers to ease paper folding.

Scrapbook - An decorative album into which photographs, notes and memories are kept and displayed.

Sleeve - Paper that has been folded and secured to house a card or invitation.

Square Knot - A type of loose, decorative knot used in paper crafting and card making.

Stencil - A sheet, in which a desired design has been cut so that ink or paint applied to the sheet will reproduce the pattern onto the surface beneath.

Stylus - An instrument, usually with a pointed, or ballpoint end, used for scoring or embossing paper.

T

Triangle - An instrument used to draw right angles. Can be used with a ruler to make angled cuts.

Toile - Refers to a French pictorial textile pattern.

V

Valentine's Day - February 14, celebrated by the exchange of valentines or love tokens. Also called Saint Valentine's Day.

Vellum - Translucent or semitranslucent paper or cardstock.

W

Watermark - A marking in paper usually produced by the pressure of projecting a design onto the paper processing roll and visible when the paper is held up to light.

Weaving - The process of forming a texture, fabric, or design by interlacing or intertwining elements.

Resources

Many of the materials in this book were manufactured by the following companies:

Anna Griffin, Inc.
733 Lambert Drive
Atlanta, GA 30324
888-817-8170
www.annagriffin.com

Artistic Wire
752 North Larch
Elmhurst, IL 60126
630-530-7567
www.artisticwire.com

Ellison, Inc.
25862 Commercentre Drive
Lake Forest, CA 92630
800-253-2238
www.ellison.com

Fiskars Brands, Inc.
Fiskars School, Office & Craft
7811 West Stewart Avenue
Wausau, WI 54401
800-950-0203
www.crafts.fiskars.com

Jo-ann's Etc.
2361 Rosecrans Ave., Suite 360
El Segundo, CA 90245
888-739-4120
www.joann.com

Kinko's
P.O. Box 1935
Provo, UT 84603-9926
www.kinkos.com
800-2-KINKOS

Michaels
8000 Bent Branch Dr.
Irving, TX 75063
800-MICHAELS
www.michaels.com

Office Depot
Corporate Support Center
2200 Old Germantown Road
Delray Beach, FL 33445
800-GO-DEPOT
www.officedepot.com

Offray Ribbon
Bomboy Lane & Ninth Street
Berwick, PA 18603
800-BERWICK
www.offray.com

Plaid Enterprises, Inc.
P.O. Box 7600
Norcross, GA 30091-7600
678-291-8100
www.plaidonline.com

Paper Style
11390 Old Roswell Road
Suite 122
Alpharetta, GA 30004
888-670-5300
www.paperstyle.com

Sam Flax
1460 Northside Drive
Atlanta, GA 30318
800-SAM-FLAX
www.samflax.com

Xacto Knife
Hunt Corporation Customer Service
P.O. Box 5819
Statesville, NC 28687
800-879-4868
www.hunt-corp.com

3M
Corporate Headquarters
3M Center
St. Paul, MN 55144-1000
888-364-3577
www.3m.com

Index

Index continued

Metric Equivalency Charts

inches to millimeters and centimeters							yards to meters										
inches	mm	cm	inches	cm	inches	cm	yards	meters	yards	meters	yards	meters	yards	meters	yards	meters
⅛	3	0.3	9	22.9	30	76.2	⅛	0.11	2⅛	1.94	4⅛	3.77	6⅛	5.60	8⅛	7.43
¼	6	0.6	10	25.4	31	78.7	⅛	0.11	2⅛	1.94	4⅛	3.77	6⅛	5.60	8⅛	7.43
½	13	1.3	12	30.5	33	83.8	¼	0.23	2¼	2.06	4¼	3.89	6¼	5.72	8¼	7.54
⅝	16	1.6	13	33.0	34	86.4	⅜	0.34	2⅜	2.17	4⅜	4.00	6⅜	5.83	8⅜	7.66
¾	19	1.9	14	35.6	35	88.9	⅝	0.46	2½	2.29	4½	4.11	6½	5.94	8½	7.77
⅞	22	2.2	15	38.1	36	91.4	⅝	0.57	2⅝	2.40	4⅝	4.23	6⅝	6.06	8⅝	7.89
1	25	2.5	16	40.6	37	94.0	¾	0.69	2¾	2.51	4¾	4.34	6¾	6.17	8¾	8.00
1¼	32	3.2	17	43.2	38	96.5	⅞	0.80	2⅞	2.63	4⅞	4.46	6⅞	6.29	8⅞	8.12
1½	38	3.8	18	45.7	39	99.1	1	0.91	3	2.74	5	4.57	7	6.40	9	8.23
1¾	44	4.4	19	48.3	40	101.6	1¼	1.03	3¼	2.86	5⅛	4.69	7⅛	6.52	9⅛	8.34
2	51	5.1	20	50.8	41	104.1	1¼	1.14	3¼	2.97	5¼	4.80	7¼	6.63	9¼	8.46
2½	64	6.4	21	53.3	42	106.7	1⅜	1.26	3⅜	3.09	5⅜	4.91	7⅜	6.74	9⅜	8.57
3	76	7.6	22	55.9	43	109.2	1½	1.37	3½	3.20	5½	5.03	7½	6.86	9½	8.69
3½	89	8.9	23	58.4	44	111.8	1⅝	1.49	3⅝	3.31	5⅝	5.14	7⅝	6.97	9⅝	8.80
4	102	10.2	24	61.0	45	114.3	1¾	1.60	3¾	3.43	5¾	5.26	7¾	7.09	9¾	8.92
4½	114	11.4	25	63.5	46	116.8	1⅞	1.71	3⅞	3.54	5⅞	5.37	7⅞	7.20	9⅞	9.03
5	127	12.7	26	66.0	47	119.4	2	1.83	4	3.66	6	5.49	8	7.32	10	9.14
6	152	15.2	27	68.6	48	121.9										
7	178	17.8	28	71.1	49	124.5										
8	203	20.3	29	73.7	50	127.0										